The Sacrament of Suffering

BOOKS BY JAMES AYLWARD MOHLER

Man Needs God: An Interpretation of Biblical Faith

The Beginning of Eternal Life: The Dynamic Faith of Thomas Aquinas, Origins, and Interpretation

Dimensions of Faith: Yesterday and Today

The Origin and Evolution of the Priesthood: A Return to the Sources

The Heresy of Monasticism: The Christian Monks—Types and Anti-Types

Cosmos, Man, God, Messiah: An Introduction to Religion

The School of Jesus: An Overview of Christian Education Yesterday and Today

Dimensions of Love: East and West

Sexual Sublimation and the Sacred

The Sacrament of Suffering

JAMES AYLWARD MOHLER

Fides/Claretian
Notre Dame, Indiana 46556

ACKNOWLEDGMENTS

Edith Stein, *The Science of the Cross,* tr. H. Graef, Chicago, Henry Regnery Co., 1960.

Marguerite-Marie Teilhard de Chardin, *L'Energie Spirituelle de la Souffrance,* Paris, Editions du Seuil, 1950.

Pierre Teilhard de Chardin, *Writings in Time of War,* tr. R. Hague, New York, Harper and Row, 1967.

Simone Weil, *Notebooks,* 2 vols., tr. A. Wills, New York, Putnam's Sons, 1956

Library of Congress Cataloging in Publication Data

Mohler, James A
  The sacrament of suffering.

  Includes bibliographical references.
  1. Suffering. I. Title.
BT732.7.M63   231'.8   79–15738
ISBN 0–8190–0632–7

7793

Contents

THE SACRAMENT OF SUFFERING
Prologue

From the beginning man has puzzled over the meaning of suffering and death. Why do babies die? Why do the good suffer? Why are young men in full bloom killed in war? Why all the pain and agony that meet him every day?

Are these punishments at the hands of a wrathful God? Or are they caused by evil spirits who are able to tempt man beyond his strength?

Hinduism says that man causes his own suffering. The iron rusts itself. So his bad karma must be worked off in this life or in the next. Buddha said that life is suffering, caused by man's own selfish desires.

Theism's remote deity seems aloof from man's distress, whereas atheism, rejecting theism's ideal absolutes, tries to solve the inequities of the world by man's own efforts. But the compassionate God of the bible and his suffering Son gave new hope to the world in travail.

We have called this book the sacrament of suffering. But how can this be? Judaism sees suffering as holy for the Shekhinah, God's compassionate Presence, hovers over the sickbed.

Christians see suffering as holy, for God sanctified it on the cross. So Christ himself is the sacrament of suffering, taking on our sins and guilt. But the Christian church is his body and so must also suffer. Christ asks his followers to share his cross and continue his passion.

And so the church also is the sacrament of suffering in which we share each other's sorrows and pains. If one suffers, all suffer. The eucharist more specifically is the sacrament of suffering, for it is the communion of the saints in the unbloody sacrifice of Christ.

If the suffering of Christ is divine and redemptive, and if we can share his cross through our pain, then suffering is truly a sacrament. This is why the eucharist heals, for it is born of the suffering of Christ.

We hope to examine the thoughts of many modern people including Bonhoeffer, Stein, Gandhi, Weil, the Teilhards, Lewis, Heschel, and others on the meaning of suffering in the twentieth century. Many experienced prison, torture, sickness, martyrdom in this sacrament of purification. But, in a sense, we are all patients, as Heschel notes, for we are not yet complete.

A common theme of the philosophers of suffering is that much pain results from a certain alienation from God or society or both. Often society casts out dissidents, but only the individual can cast off God.

The avoidance of suffering is man's greatest concern. Witness the billion dollar medical industry. But modern science has not solved the problem of man's anguish. It may cover it up or block it temporarily with drugs, surgery, or other therapy. But the true meaning of suffering lies deeper, in a suffering God, who made man's sin and pain significant by taking them on himself.

I

DIETRICH BONHOEFFER
The Price of Discipleship

Communion of the Saints

Dietrich Bonhoeffer, brilliant theologian of the German Confessing Church and firm opponent of Nazi cruelty, sees the cross of Christ as the sign of the true Christian.

In his very first book, *Communion of the Saints,*[1] he follows his mentor, Luther, and turns to the gospels to find the paradigm of the Christian community of brotherly concern.

The Christian loves his fellows as Christ loves him and as the Father loves Christ. And as Christ has compassion on us, so we should put our neighbor in our place, loving him in lieu of ourselves. Hallmarks of the communion of the saints are togetherness and acting for each other (126).

Where one member is, the church is. God acts through us to our neighbor, bearing each other's burdens, transformed into each other in love. "The infirmities and sins of my neighbor afflict me as if they were my own, as Christ was afflicted by our sins" (127).

If I fail, the church comes to help me. And when I die, Christ comes with the communion of the saints to suffer

---

1. New York, Harper and Row, 1963.

and die with me. We do not walk our path of sorrow alone, but accompanied by Christ and his church.

Where one man or woman is, the communion of saints is. And where the communion of saints is, Christ is. As Christ bears our burdens, we should bear his and our neighbor's. This is Holy Communion, the Body of Christ as the sacrament of shared suffering. Each becomes Christ for the other. One man's chastity helps another's sexual tensions. Prayer and fasting aid others. Vicarious suffering goes back to the Suffering Servant, Jesus and Paul, and it is required of the Christian.

No man is saved alone. The lifeblood of the church is prayer for one another. I enter into the other's sorrow and guilt and his sins and infirmity weigh me down (133).

The church takes on the sins of the brethren as Christ bore them on the cross. Christ, as the communion of saints, forgives sins for he bore them.

When Adam sinned, he destroyed creatureliness to be like God. In our sinful sexuality, we destroy the creatureliness of the other, violating that person in thought, word or deed.[2]

In his flight from God, Adam fell from unity to division, the one becoming two. He hides from God because he is God.

The story of Genesis is both a curse and a promise. The enmity of the serpent in the pain of childbirth, the burden of labor and death. But there is a promise of victory. While he crushes the serpent's head, his heel is wounded. "The battle for the word of God marks him with scars. . . . Locked in battle, ever newly victorious and ever newly wounded and all his kind with him"(85).

2. Dietrich Bonhoeffer, *Creation and Fall,* London, SCM, 1960, p. 80.

Man and nature are enemies. When man tries to rise above other creatures to be like God, they withdraw. Yet nature continues to sustain him.

Cain, the first born on the cursed ground, murders Abel. Christ on the cross is the murdered Son of God and the end of the story. Man dies, but Christ lives, and the tree of life becomes the cross of Christ.

It is only a weak and suffering God, who can conquer the suffering of Adam. Christ takes on sinful flesh. "Humility is made necessary by the world under the curse."[3] The weak Christ, a beggar among beggars, despairing among the despairing, dying among the dying, made sin for us, crucified for sinners, bearing our sins.

The humiliated God-Man is a stumbling block, but we must see through the scandal to be saved. The communion of saints must be humble with the humble Christ.

To Die in Christ

Bonhoeffer taught his seminarians at Finkenwalde to foster a community spirit according to the gospels.

Though Christianity had been tough in the early days of the martyrs and monks, over the millenia it had become weak and easy. No more bearing the cross of Christ. In fact, modern Christianity is probably the easiest of all world religions.

In his *Cost of Discipleship* (1937),[4] he explains that the modern Christian really has little to do, for he gets cheap grace, paid in advance through the sacraments. Instead of

3. Dietrich Bonhoeffer, *Christ the Center* (1933), New York, Harper and Row, 1966, p. 111.
4. New York, Macmillan, 1965.

taking up the cross of Christ, the Christian now sits back at his ease enjoying abundant graces. Forgiveness without repentance, baptism without discipline, communion without confession, grace without the cross, grace without Jesus Christ, living and incarnate.

Costly grace, on the other hand, is the treasure hidden in a field, or the pearl of great price. Christ calls us to pluck out our eye if it scandalizes and to leave all to follow him.

Costly grace costs a man his life, for it cost God the life of his Son. It condemns sin and justifies the sinner. "What has cost God much, cannot be cheap for us" (48). Costly grace is God's word of forgiveness to a broken and contrite heart.

Martyrdom and monasticism were costly grace, but martyrdom became rare and monasticism turned weak and worldly. Luther taught that costly grace is for all, not just the monks. But his followers were not enthusiastic. Only one who has left all is truly justified. Jesus Christ is the narrow and hard way. Cheap grace only closes the way to Christ and makes us weak.

Jesus must suffer, for he cannot be Christ without suffering. "So the disciple is a disciple only insofar as he shares his Lord's suffering and rejection and crucifixion. Discipleship means adherence to the law of Christ which is the law of the cross" (96).

To follow Christ, one must deny himself. "To endure the cross is not a tragedy, it is the suffering which is the fruit of an exclusive allegiance to Christ" (97). Discipleship means sharing the suffering and death of Christ to the fullest. No need to ask for or search for the cross. God has one waiting for us.

Discipleship means abandoning ourselves to Christ on the cross. This is not the end of our life, but the beginning of our union with Christ. "When Christ calls a man, he bids him come and die." This is the death of the old man with all his affections and lusts.

As Christ shares his cross with his disciples, so the Christian must bear the sins of others, but supported by Christ. Bearing my brother's burdens. "The call to follow Christ means a call to share the work of forgiving men their sins. Forgiveness is the Christ-like suffering which it is the Christian's duty to bear" (100).

The church is the sacrament of suffering and so suffering is the sign of the true church. If we reject the cross of Christ, we lose our fellowship with Christ and no longer follow him. We must lose our lives to find them in him.

The exact opposite of discipleship is to be ashamed of the cross of Christ. To bear one's cross is the only way to conquer suffering, for this is the way that Christ defeated it. The cup of suffering will only pass by drinking it.

If suffering is alienation from God, then one joined to God cannot suffer. Jesus Christ takes on the suffering of the world, man's alienation from God. And when he drinks this large cup, suffering passes over him. Suffering has to be endured to pass away.

Blessed are the mourners. Sorrow does not wear the disciples down or break them. "They bear their sorrow in the strength of him who bears them up, who bore the whole suffering of the world upon the cross" (122).

Blessed are the persecuted. When the disciples renounce the world for Christ, the world is offended and so persecutes and rejects them. The world finds them repulsive, menacing, weak, patient, silent, and so wants to get rid of them. They will have their reward in heaven (128).

The way to destroy evil is not by resistance which causes more evil. "Evil becomes a spent force when we put up no resistance" (158).

In fellowship with Christ in his crucified and glorified body we take up his cross. "The body of Christ, which was given for us, which suffered the punishment of our sins, makes us free to take our share of suffering and death 'for Christ!'" (273).

Christ left some suffering for his church, his tortured body. "God grants one man the grace to bear special suffering in place of another. And this suffering must at all costs be endured and overcome" (274). Christians die daily in the war between the flesh and the spirit. And when they are insulted, they are conformed to the humiliated Christ.

Temptations are a special type of suffering and tension at the battle line of the flesh and the spirit.[5] In my temptations of the flesh I share in the death of Jesus in the flesh, but raised in the spirit.

Suffering is a temptation of Satan to separate us from God. Why me? This is the story of Job. Yet suffering can lead us to a knowledge of our sins and help us return to God.

Suffering is really the suffering of Christ in us. "The deeper a man is driven into suffering, the nearer he comes to Christ." Temptation is a voluntary suffering for the sake of righteousness. Suffering for Christ's sake is a judgment on sin.

The psalms are songs of suffering. If I am guilty, why

5. Dietrich Bonhoeffer, *Temptation* (1937), New York, Macmillan, 1956, pp. 34–38.

does God not forgive me? If not guilty, why does he torture me? (Ps 38, 44, 79).[6] Divine suffering is the answer. God enters into our suffering through Jesus Christ (Ps 23, 37). The imprecatory psalms lead us to the cross of Christ and the forgiveness of our enemies.

Paul tells us we should bear each other's burdens. Bonhoeffer makes this the leitmotif at Finkenwalde.[7] "It is only when he is a burden that another person is really a brother and not merely an object to be manipulated." The burden of men was so great that God had to endure the cross.

As a mother bears her child, so God takes men on himself and they weigh him to the ground. As Christ bore our griefs and sorrows, we should bear each other's. "The fellowship of the cross is to experience the burden of the others." Strength and weakness in fellowship (Eph 4/2).

But sin breaks up the fellowship. However, as Christ bore our sins, we should be tolerant of each other's faults. "Since every sin of each member burdens and indicts the whole community, the congregation rejoices, in the midst of all pain and the burden the brother's sin inflicts, that it is the privilege of bearing and forgiving." The cross gives us the strength we need.

Sin is darkness and alienation. But in confession it is brought to light. The confessing sinner is no longer alone. "He stands in the fellowship of sinners who live by the grace of God in the cross of Jesus Christ." In order to reenter the congregation, one must confess to another

6. Dietrich Bonhoeffer, *The Psalms*, Minneapolis, Augsburg, 1970, p. 48.

7. Dietrich Bonhoeffer, *Life Together*, (1939), New York, Harper and Row, 1954, pp. 100–113.

who acts in lieu of the community. In the humiliation of
confession we share the humble sinner's death of Jesus
Christ.

Drinking the Cup

In 1943 Bonhoeffer was imprisoned for his complicity
in the plot against Hitler. Only one who has suffered can
speak of suffering. In his *Ethics* (1943–45)[8] he teaches the
place of suffering on the road to liberation. Self-discipline,
action, suffering, death, liberation. What a transformation! The hands, once powerful and free, are now tied.
"You yielded your freedom into the hands of God that he
might perfect you in glory" (15).

Though man fled God in the fall, God brings him back
in the cross. It is only through the cross that we can understand what his love is and overcome our alienation.
Though tormented by the world, he forgives it and takes
on its guilt.

Jesus is the merciful "yes" of him who has compassion,
suffering to the end man's fate (41). Jesus Christ is not A
man, but MAN. So what happens to him, happens to all. It
is only in the light of the incarnation that we can know real
man with all his faults and not despise him. Christ becoming man, took on man's faults.

What happened to Christ, happens to every man in him.
"Only the crucified man is at peace with God. . . . To be
taken up by God and executed on the cross and reconciled,
that is the reality of manhood" (75).

To most people the crucifixion appears to be folly and

8. New York, Macmillan, 1965.

failure. But success is the measure of the world where it justifies evil and covers up guilt. However, neither success nor jealousy of success can ultimately overcome the world. Only Christ under God's sentence can conquer. "In the cross of Christ, God confronts the successful man with the sanctification of pain, sorrow, humiliation, failure, poverty, loneliness, and despair" (77).

God's acceptance of the cross is his judgment on success. The unsuccessful man does not stand before God because of his failure, but only because of his willing acceptance of the cross given him by divine love.

The Christian must be formed on the model of the crucified, sentenced by God. "In his daily existence man carries with him God's sentence of death, the necessity of dying before God for the sake of sin."

Man dies daily in his sins. "Humbly he bears the scars on his body and soul, the marks of the wounds which sin inflicts on him" (81).

So the Christian cannot look down on sinners, for he also is at fault. Others he can excuse, but not himself. And his suffering enables him to accept God's judgment. Stamped with Christ's image in his suffering, the Christian lives in Christ, life in death, light in darkness.

In his *Letters From Prison* (1943–45)[9] Bonhoeffer notes the tendency to place man on a pedestal, overlooking his frailty. "We must form our estimate of men less from their achievements and failures and more from their sufferings" (24).

Often one who has not suffered is insensitive to the pain of others. Christ seized suffering willingly and bore our sins as if they were his own. The Christian should share

9. New York, Macmillan, 1966.

Christ's sympathy. He cannot wait till he experiences suffering first. No! "The sufferings of his brethren for whom Christ died are enough to awaken his active sympathy" (30).

Dietrich suffered intensely in his imprisonment for he had gloried in freedom, mobility, love of nature. Suffering is easier under command than when freely assumed. Moreover, it is easier to suffer with others than alone, and easier to suffer as a public hero than in ignominy. It is easier to die physically than to endure spiritual pain. Christ's cross was free, abandoned, ignominious in both body and soul.

Bonhoeffer served as chaplain for his fellow prisoners. In his morning prayer on Christmas, 1944, he believes that the Lord will not lay on him more than he can bear. "Lord Jesus Christ, you were poor and in misery, a captive and forsaken, as I am. You know all man's distress, you abide with me when all others have deserted me" (88).

He asks God's help in his misery for he misses his loved ones very much. "All we can do is to wait patiently. We must suffer the unutterable agony of separation, and feel the longing until it makes us sick" (111).

The prisoners suffered severely during the night bombings, which Bonhoeffer sees as God's wrath turning man to himself. However, he does not waste his time philosophizing. "It seems to me more important that we should really experience certain kinds of distress, rather than try to bottle it up or explain it away" (130).

Resistance or submission? Both are necessary. Defy fate, yet submit when the time comes. How can we find the "They"(God) in the "It"(fate)? And how does fate become Providence (146)?

We should rejoice when something affects us deeply and

accept any accompanying suffering as a soul-enriching high tension between heaven and earth, giving off big sparks (157).

In his prison meditations, Bonhoeffer mulls over the problem of a religion in which people only fly to God when all else fails, for when man is strong and prosperous he does not need God. But God cannot be just a stopgap until modern science conquers man's problems and sufferings. No, God must be found at the center and not at the edge of existence, in life and not just in death, in health as well as in illness (190).

The Christian must drink Christ's cup of lees. "And only in his doing that is the crucified and risen Lord with him, and he crucified and risen with Christ" (206).

Why does God hide when we need him? He even abandoned his own Son on the cross. The hidden God teaches us that we must learn to get along without him. "The God who is with us is the God who forsakes us" (Mk 15/34). God allows himself to be edged out of the world and onto the cross. It is not by his omnipotence that Christ helps us, but by his weakness and suffering (219).

Bonhoeffer feels restless and sick, as a bird in a cage, weary and empty at prayer. Is he like an army fleeing victory (221)?

The difference between Christians and unbelievers is that Christians unite themselves to a suffering God. "Man is challenged to participate in the suffering of God at the hands of a godless world." So the true follower of Christ must participate in the suffering of God in the world (222-23).

Whereas men of the world fly to God when they are suffering, the Christian stands by his grieving God. Bonhoeffer's worldly Christian takes life in stride with its pains and gains. "We throw ourselves utterly in the arms of God and participate in his suffering in the world and watch with Christ at Gethsemane" (226).

Personal asceticism can rob suffering of its reliance on divine command. Deliverance is placing our cause in God's hands. All is possible with God, and danger only drives us closer to him. He alone gives meaning to suffering and death.

New Year's Day, 1945. "Should it be ours to drain the cup of grieving even to the dregs of pain, at thy command we will not falter, thankfully receiving all that is given by your loving hand" (249). When called by the executioner, Dietrich whispered to a friend, "For me this is the beginning of life."

Bonhoeffer followed Paul and Luther in his theology of suffering. The Christian must shoulder the cross of Christ. And as Christ bore our sins, we should take on each other's faults in loving forgiveness in the Communion of Saints.

God is not someone we fly to as a last resort, rather he is at our deepest center where storms and trials cannot reach.

II

EDITH STEIN
The Science of the Cross

Empathy

Edith Stein also suffered under the Nazis. She showed an early concern for the pains of others in her dissertation on empathy under Husserl at Freiburg (1917).[1]

When a friend tells me that he has lost his brother, I am aware of pain. But where is the pain? It is a kind of foreign consciousness of man or god. "As a believer, he grasps the love, anger, and the command of his God in this way, and God can grasp man's life in no other way" (11).

Some say empathy is an imitation or transference of feeling, perceiving the other "I" in my "I."

Sensual empathy is a "sensing in." "I interpret it as a sensing, living body and empathically project myself into it. I obtain a new image of the spatial world and a new zero point of orientation" (57). We no longer consider our own zero point as *the* zero point, but as one spatial point among many.

The phenomena of life: growth, age, health, sickness, are coseen in the living body. "We bring this cointended foreign experience to fulfillment by carrying it out with

1. Edith Stein, *On the Problem of Empathy*, The Hague, Nijhoff, 1964, tr. W. Stein.

13

him empathically" (63). "I look at this state in the other and bring it to givenness to myself in empathic projection" (65).

Empathy can help diagnose disease. For example, a doctor can empathize with his patient, looking for the cause of his illness.

The sufferings or moods of another can affect us empathically. Thus we can comprehend his bodily expression by projecting ourselves into his foreign living body. "When I empathize the pain of the injured in looking at a wound I tend to look at his face to have my experience confirmed in his expression of suffering" (78).

When I experience great pain or joy, I become aware of my suffering and the place it has in my "I." This is not perception, but experience. Pain and pleasure are experiences on the surface of the "I."

As Dilthey, Stein feels that we can empathize better with people similar to us. "How much of his experiential structure I can bring to my fulfilling intuition depends on my own structure" (104).

One may empathize even though it may conflict with his own experience. For example, though I am skeptical, I witness another sacrifice himself for his faith. "I see him behave this way and empathize a value experiencing as the motive for his conduct." This way one can gain empathically a type of "homo religiosus" which is quite foreign to him (105-5).

Stein finds a significance of empathy for the constitution of our own person. Through our empathy with related subjects what is sleeping in us is developed. Later Edith would empathize with the suffering John of the Cross and with her own persecuted people.

Moreover, it is possible to empathize negatively with different personalities. It is clear, then, what we are not. "When we empathically run into ranges of value locked to us, we become conscious of our own deficiencies" (105).

Stein leaves the question of experiencing purely mental persons such as God, or the question of religious consciousness till later. Indeed, she would spend the rest of her life pursuing this intimate empathic divine union.

Teresa Benedicta of the Cross

By 1922 Edith had experienced God. As she writes in her work on the philosophical foundation of psychology.

> There is a certain state of resting in God, of a complete relaxation of all mental effort, when one no longer makes any plans or decisions, where one no longer acts, but abandons all the future to the divine will.[2]

She was baptized in 1922, much against her mother's wishes. Austere and recollected, she lived as a nun while teaching in a convent school at Speyer, where she served as a spiritual adviser to both students and nuns.

As if forseeing her own passion, Edith writes to one of her spiritual daughters (7/4/31).[3] "The Lord must have some special design for you because he makes you pass through so hard a school."

Silent, recollected, prayerful, and studious, Edith impressed all with her great sanctity. She spent much time before the Blessed Sacrament in quiet comtemplation.

2. Hilda Graef, *The Scholar and the Cross*, Westminster, Newman, 1955, p. 30.

3. Hilda Graef, *The Scholar and the Cross*, p. 90.

As Hitler gained more power, she saw inevitable suffering ahead. Thus she writes in 1932, "Christ continues to live and to suffer in his members, and the suffering borne in union with him is his suffering, integrated and made fruitful in his great redemptive work."

As Hitler stepped up his persecution of the Jews, Edith saw her own people helping bear the cross of Christ, their fellow Jew. Facing the worst as a true prophetess, Edith offers herself as a sacrifice for her people.

At last, she had the permission of her spiritual father, Abbot Walzer, to join Carmel, preparing to give up all, even her love of scholarship. "Human activity cannot help us, but only the passion of Christ. My desire is to share in that."[4]

But her mother needs her now more than ever, so she is torn between her mother and her vocation in a tension of the cross. But she must step out into the darkness of faith with all its suffering and uncertainty. Though she wanted to offer herself for her own, they misunderstood, thinking rather that she had abandoned them.

In the Cologne Carmel, John of the Cross, her holy founder, was her inspiration. Todo y nada. A rejection of all that is not God. All she wants is to be a victim in the name of Israel.

Now Sister Teresa Benedicta of the Cross, she sees the shadow of Calvary on the crib of the baby Jesus. The star of Bethlehem shines in the dark night. The second day of Christmas is the color of blood and the third day is mourning. "The crib of the child is surrounded by martyrs."[5]

But where is the peace that the infant brought? Not all

4. Ibid., p. 100.
5. *Writings of Edith Stein*, selected and translated by H. Graef, Westminster, Newman, 1956, p. 22.

are of good will, so there is no amity. Jesus is a stumbling block to the children of darkness. And their night of sin appears blacker against the light of Christ. Those who come to him are the laborers and the burdened, shepherds and kings.

"Do not hesitate to take upon yourselves the sufferings and hardships his service entails," as the Holy Innocents followed Jesus to their death. We have to be prepared to accept all from God, for he alone knows what is good for us, be it want, failure, or humiliation. "If we do this, we can live for the present without being burdened by the future" (27).

If we belong to Christ, we must live his life, including the cross. "And all sufferings that come from without are as nothing compared with the dark night of the soul, when the divine light no longer shines and the voice of the Lord no longer speaks." Why is God silent?

Christ is both God and man, his human nature enabling him to suffer and die, while his divine nature gives his suffering and death infinite redemptive power.

> Christ's suffering and death are continued in his mystical body and in each of his members. Every man must suffer and die. But if he is a living member of the body of Christ, his suffering and death will receive redemptive power from the divinity of the head. This is the objective reason why the saints have desired to suffer (27).

So one united with Christ will remain tranquil even in the depths of the dark night of abandonment. Perhaps God is using my agony to help another.

We need daily contact with God to know his will for us. For he knows our weaknesses and gives his help accordingly. We follow the unity of his mysteries from the crib to the cross and resurrection. "In his company the way of every one of us, indeed of all mankind, leads through suffering and death to this same glorious goal" (31).

If the Word is to become flesh, the virgin must become a mother. And if the soul of Christ is to live on in his disciple, the bowl of Benedicta's contemplation must overflow to others. The virgin is a type of the church, the bride of Christ, and so must suffer and die with him.

Benedicta returned to her scholarship, writing *Finite and Infinite Being*.[6] As Augustine, she sees the reflection of the Trinity in creation. But one must live in his depths to perceive the divine image. Small inconveniences do not bother the deep person. The more recollected one is, the more he will radiate to others.

The soul surrenders herself to God's will which engenders the Son in her. Uniting herself to the Son, the soul disappears in him so that the Father sees only his Son. Their life unites with the Holy Spirit and pours out love. The Trinity is also reflected in the community, but in a less perfect manner because of the imperfect union.

As Hitler increases his persecutions, Benedicta anticipates her own passion and it pains her that her own Aryan sisters continue to vote for the man. For her safety Benedicta is exiled to Holland where she guides many souls in her unique empathic manner. Every soul is different in God's eyes. "He alone knows the secret efforts as well as the obstacles that every soul must overcome."[7]

She also kept up her exploration into mystical theology, clearing the way for God who is the first theologian. "All speaking about God presupposes God's own speaking. His

6. *Endliches und Ewiges Sein, Edith Steins Werke, Band* II, Freiburg, Herder, 1962.
7. Hilda Graef, *Scholar and the Cross*, p. 199.

most real speaking is that before which human speech is silenced."[8] God, the first theologian, speaks the divine Word. And the Word made flesh is his first utterance.

Delightful Wounds

As the date of her crucifixion approaches, Benedicta is asked to write a commentary on the 400th anniversary of her founder, John of the Cross' birthday.[9] As her mentor, Benedicta, too, feels the weight of the cross, the sweet pain of the master's call. Through the years many sorrows had been hers from Husserl's lack of appreciation to racial slurs, to her mother's misunderstanding of her vocation and her final trials under the Nazis.

But if one is to be a bride of Christ, she must be willing to be stripped naked and nailed to a cross beside her divine Groom. Her stripping and humiliation began early in her life and by progressive stages would lead to the final holocaust in the gas chambers and crematories of Brzezince.

John of the Cross had been persecuted by members of his own order which he was trying to reform. As a true prophet he was rewarded with jail, starvation, and painful scourgings in the refectory.

When John wrote of the dark night, it was from personal experience. This night is an absence of light, invisible and formless. Our senses are useless in this black which is a foretaste of death. But the night also brings peace, solitude, silence, rest.

8. Hilda Graef, *Scholar and the Cross*, p. 95.
9. Edith Stein, *Science of the Cross*, tr. H. Graef, Chicago, Regnery, 1960.

John passed through this dark night to the light of
union with God. The way of faith is a dark knowledge
compared with the clarity of natural reason. We know, but
we cannot see.

> As long as we are on earth, God remains hidden from us
> even in the most blissful union. Because our spiritual eye is
> not adapted to his too radiant light, it seems to look into the
> darkness of night (31).

The night has different shades of black. Faith is mid-
night, extremely dark, for it takes away both senses and
reason. "But when the soul finds God, it is as if the dawn of
the new day of eternity were already breaking into its
night."

The active night of the senses imitates the cross in
mortification. Now all that people desire: health, wealth,
and fame seem as darkness in the divine light. John's
squelching of desire before the holy enlightening reminds
one of the teachings of Siddhartha Gautama.

The passive night of the cross is a divine gift in which the
soul no longer finds joy in creatures and is fearful lest it
displease God. And God no longer communicates himself
through the senses.

Though it feels abandoned by God because it no longer
experiences sensual joys, the soul should surrender itself
to dark contemplation which is a peaceful and loving infu-
sion of God, inflaming the soul in a spirit of love.

But in the beginning, aridity, emptiness, anxiety, fear
and a powerful longing for God. By this wound of love
God gradually detaches the soul from the senses, leading it
to the spirit (36-7).

> The dark night becomes the school of all the virtues. To
> remain faithful to the spiritual life without finding consola-

tion and refreshment in it is a training in resignation and patience. Thus the soul attains to a pure love of God, acting solely for his sake (37).

But the soul endures further storms and temptations, for the higher the union, the more purification is needed. But there is still light and hope of resurrection.

The night of the spirit is darker and intenser, depriving the soul of the light of natural reason, a stripping of the memory, intellect, and will by hope, faith, and love. "To drink the chalice with the Lord (Mt 20/22) means to die to nature in matters of sense as well as spiritually. Only thus can one ascend by the narrow way" (43).

This is not through consoling meditations and spiritual delights, but through the cross. Even Christ was abandoned by his Father on the cross.

The spirit must annihilate itself spiritually as well as sensually.

> When it is reduced to nothing in the most profound humiliation, then the spiritual union with God comes to pass, which is the highest stage the soul can reach on this earth.

This is not spiritual delight, but living death on the cross (*Ascent of Mt. Carmel* 2/7) (44).

Faith is a darkness, a cloud, that leads to God. It resembles God insofar as it blinds human reason and appears as darkness. When the soul is no longer interested in discursive thought or in other creatures and only wants to remain quietly in the Lord, it is ready for the dark night and the divine touch by way of the cross.

John of the Cross followed Christ in his suffering and death, not through consolations and locutions. "It is a real crucifixion to suspend the life of the spirit and to take away from it all its refreshment" (58). When two people are really in love, they do not need words for they just want to rest peacefully in each other. The cross is the staff for climbing Mt. Carmel. "For Christ accomplished his greatest work, the reconciliation and union of mankind with God, in the utmost humiliation and annihilation on the cross" (89). The soul must emulate this humiliation in the darkness of faith, as God blinds the understanding.

Aridity, distaste, pain, and spiritual crucifixion. The soul feels cast out by God and purged of all sensual and spiritual joys. This is not just night, but anguish and torture as well. "The pain and torment of the soul is caused by the fact that the divine infused contemplation contains a wealth of sublime perfection" (91). This is true especially if the soul is not yet purified for the dark night shows the soul clearly its many sins.

> When divine contemplation melts the human soul, God consumes and destroys the spiritual substance of the soul and envelops it in such deep black darkness that it believes itself to be given over to destruction and dissolution by a cruel spiritual death. (92)

God humbles the soul in order to raise it. "As long as the Lord has not completed the purification as it pleases him, there is no means or remedy to soothe its pain" (93). This goes on until the soul is humbled and purification may last for years. At times the dark night can be illuminating and liberating, but the soul in purgation feels that the pain will never end.

To be born again the soul must be purged by a spiritual burning, "An infused love which shows itself in suffering rather than in action" (98). The soul is inflamed and wounded by love.

> If a man refuses to enter the night in order to seek the Beloved, to deny his self-will and die to himself, if he wants to seek him only on the bed of comfort.... he will never find him.

The soul ascending to God, must go deep within itself. John of the Cross calls God the deepest center or point of rest of the soul. But the soul cannot descend by itself.

Indwelling demands interior being on both sides, to be able to receive another being within itself, united, yet independent. To effect divine union, the soul must be completely empty (132). In my mystical union God touches my interior and opens his own being to me. The source of divine life touches the source of the life of the soul. God is present, though hidden.

> The soul is now seized by the felt presence of God, or, in those experiences of the dark night in which the soul is deprived of his felt presence, that it is painfully wounded with the fervent desire that remains if God withdraws from the soul (137).

The living flame of love touches and purifies the soul in a divine cautery. The soul delights in being transformed into God. This sweet burn causes a delightful wound and the soul is purified. Sometimes the wound can be seen externally in stigmata.

"The flame of divine life touches the soul with the very tenderness of this life and wounds it so deeply that it wholly dissolves in love" (142).

A sweet burn, delectable wound, a firebrand of love

cauterizing the lacerations of misery and sin, "healing them and changing them into wounds of love." The wound keeps enlarging until the soul is one great trauma and yet made whole again. "It is wholly wounded and wholly healed" (148).

God chastises softly. "You have wounded me in order to heal me, O divine Hand" (John)(150). The divine Son is the Father's delicate touch, a foretaste of eternal life where the soul will be rewarded for all of its pain and suffering. So many want the road to glory paved with consolation, but suffering is the only way.

In his *Spiritual Canticle* John of the Cross asks God where he has hidden himself. He feels the sorrow of a lover who has been allowed to feel the happy presence of the beloved, but now must be without him (179).

Burning touches of love wound the soul and leave it burnt out. Thus consumed by the flame, it is renewed as the Phoenix (180).

Once the soul has been touched by God, it can find peace in nothing else. "There is nowhere a medicine for the wounds of love save with him who has inflicted them." So the wounded soul runs after her Beloved who lifts her up in spiritual betrothal.

Though the soul is lured back to the world, the Lord removes all distractions to permanent union. Intoxicated with love, the soul's eyes lock with the eyes of her Beloved. "But he, too, is wounded. For between lovers the wound of one is common to both and both have one and the same feeling" (185).

When the soul enjoys the presence of her Beloved, she no longer cries out in longing. And he adorns her in majesty, divine knowledge, and glory. All the labors and sufferings of the day are over.

But the devil still fights this divine contemplation with

sensual desires, disturbing both body and soul, causing a tension of spiritual anxiety. The soul suffers on because she is not yet in full control (189).

The sufferings of the dark night share in the dark night of Christ at Gethsemane. The longing desire for the hidden God permeates the whole mystical way.

"But no human pain of desire can be compared with the suffering of the God-man who possessed the Beatific Vision throughout his life," until he gave it up at Gethsemane, utterly abandoned by God. As man, he suffers. As God, he grasps fully the deprived Vision.

Fallen human nature can be raised up by God. "This happens 'under the tree of the cross' as the fruit of Christ's death on the cross and the soul's own share in it" (195). Man fell by a tree and is raised by one. "The soul, united to Christ, gains the knowledge of good and evil through suffering with the wounded savior, purified by the sharp pain of self-knowledge" (195).

Mystical union is a share in the incarnation. "Each time a soul surrenders to him so completely that he can raise it to the mystical union, he once more becomes man, as it were" (196). One, yet two. They are members of his body and so "Endure not their own sufferings, but the passion of Christ."

In the inner wine cellar, the soul drinks of her Beloved and dissolves in love, equalizing subject and object. John comments. "Great is the power and vehemence of love since it knows how to take captive and wound God himself" (200). The soul wants to penetrate deeply into the interior of God.

> To attain this, it would be a comfort and joy to it to take upon itself all the trials and suffering of the world and it would agree to all that might aid it to this end, however

difficult and painful it might be.... In suffering it (the soul) finds its greatest delight and its highest gain, because it is a means to penetrate more deeply into the delights and depths of the wisdom of God (200).

Suffering purifies and purity deepens knowledge. So the soul is not content with ordinary suffering.

But wants to take upon itself the agonies of death . . . as a means . . . to see God. When will men realize that the depths of wisdom and the infinite riches of God are inaccessible to the soul unless it takes upon itself the fullness of suffering, unless it longs for this and finds its consolation in it?

The soul who wants true wisdom must first begin to penetrate into the depth of the suffering of the cross. This is the narrow gate.

As in nature, so in us transformation is never free of pain. Two in one flesh, God and the soul. "All life in the flesh is struggle and suffering" (205).

The more perfectly the soul grows, the more completely it surrenders to God, "The darker the night and the more painful the death." And the new man has the marks of Christ's passion on his body (205). The soul is created for divine union, but only through the cross.

In Benedicta's commentary on John of the Cross, it is at times difficult to discern who is speaking, for they are brother and sister in divine empathy.

As the Nazis close in, Benedicta and her sister Rosa near their own crucifixion. When the Gestapo summons them, they reply: "Praised be Jesus Christ!" instead of "Heil Hitler!" They were issued yellow stars of David to wear at all times.

When the Dutch bishops objected to Nazi cruelty to the

Jews, they retaliated with a pogrom against all non-Aryan
Catholics in Holland. Benedicta and Rosa were arrested
immediately (8/4/42). Taken to Westerbork, they were
brutally beaten with rifle butts and given little food.

Benedicta in her calm and peaceful manner washed and
fed wandering children who had been left by their distraught parents. She impressed all in the camp with her
sorrowful silence as the Pieta or Rachel weeping for her
children.

Benedicta and Rosa were then taken to Brzezince near
Auschwitz (8/9/42) where they were ordered to undress in
preparation for the gas chambers.

This is the moment Benedicta had prepared for all her
life. Obediently she removed her shoes, stockings, veil,
habit and underwear, placing them neatly in their proper
piles. Now naked, Benedicta and Rosa hold hands as they
walk confidently to meet their Beloved. Their white backs
bear the cruel bruises from the Nazi rifle beatings.

Benedicta had lived the passion of Christ in prayer,
mortification, fasting, and humiliation, preparing for this
last stripping. Brzezince is merely the final nailing of her
bare bruised body to the cross of Christ. Now only remains
her glorious union with her risen Groom. What Paul and
John of the Cross had written, Benedicta now teaches by
example. There is no divine union without stripping and
crucifixion.

As she had wished, Benedicta died for her people for it
was in retaliation against the Dutch bishops' protests over
Nazi cruelty to the Jews that she was killed.

III

MAHATMA GANDHI
Ahimsa

Mahatma Gandhi was also a martyr for his people. As many of his Indian predecessors such as Mahavira, Gautama, Patanjali, and Krishna, Gandhi, too, seeks a way to alleviate the vast sufferings of mankind.

Gandhi is both simple and complex. He is simple in his selfless union with universal Truth, Satya. It is alienation from Truth which is the source of suffering. One with the Self, he is joined with all other men in the Self and so empathic in their sorrows.

Gandhi's complexity is really another side of his simplicity for he is open to all religious traditions, seeing in them different manifestations of the one Truth. Though raised in Hindu and especially Jain ways, Gandhi read the New Testament, Koran, Tolstoy, Thoreau, and others.

Gandhi is supersensitive to injustice or untruth, asatya. For example, the plight of the untouchables and the cruelty of child marriages in India and the prejudice of the whites against the coolies in South Africa and India.

Gandhi is called Mahatma, Great-Souled One, who is one with Atman and so with all men. But how can a saint be involved in political action, passive resistance, strikes and the like? Gandhi answers: How can a man of God not be concerned with community injustice? "Those who say that religion has nothing to do with politics do not know what religion means."[1]

Satya

Gandhi called his movement for social justice, Satyagraha, the pursuit of Truth. In Hinduism the Supreme One is called Sat or Satya, Truth, Reality, Being. All else is Maya, illusion or untruth.

Gandhi pursued Truth in his own life by his honesty, fidelity to his wife, and loyalty to his vows. He had to seek Truth in his own person before he could quest it for others.

Truth is God. "I worship God as Truth only. I have not yet found him, but I am seeking after him." And he will sacrifice all, even himself for that.[2]

If we had already attained Truth, we would no longer be seeking it, for we would be one with God. So our religion is imperfect, searching, evolving. Gandhi feels that as there is one God, Truth, so only one religion with many manifestations (AMB 67/45).

Gandhi's search for social justice and his battle against suffering are one with his quest for Truth.

> When you want to find Truth as God, the only inevitable means is love, that is, nonviolence. And since I believe that ultimately the means and ends are convertible terms, I should not hesitate to say that God is love (AMB 70/59).

1. *Gandhi's Autobiography,* tr. M. Desai, Washington, Public Affairs Press, 1948, p. 615. (A)
2. *All Men are Brothers,* ed. K. Kipalani, New York, Columbia University Press and UNESCO, 1969, p. 66, n. 43. (AMB)

In Hinduism to attain moksha, salvation, liberation from Maya and Samsara, the individual self, jiva, must disappear, melting into Satya or Atman. "If you would swim on the bosom of the ocean of Truth, you must reduce yourself to zero" (AMB 71/61). Gandhi feels that Truth lies in the simple, lowly, the poor, the humiliated with deflated egos. So he identifies and empathizes with them. Beauty reflects Truth, whether in a person, face, art or literature. A face is only beautiful which mirrors a truthful soul. Even natural beauty points to the Truth-Creator.

"To see the universal and all-pervading Spirit of Truth face to face, one must be able to love the meanest of creatures as oneself" (A 615). Gandhi finds Truth in the despised, the untouchables. And his self-purification and self-effacement widen his soul till it embraces all the lowly—Mahatma.

Satya, Truth, is the foundation stone of his ashram,[3] as he writes from prison in 1930.

The first vow of his ashram is Satya. Why? Because the very purpose of the community is to pursue and practice Truth (Satyagraha). Truth is the very life and breath of the ashram, it is the basis of all other rules and principles of life. Truth in thought, word and action. Outside of Truth there is no knowledge or inward peace.

But this is not the easy way!

> The quest of Truth involves tapas, self-suffering, sometimes even death. There can be no place in it for even a trace of self-interest. In such selfless search for Truth nobody can lose his bearings for long.

3. *Nonviolent Resistance* (Satyagraha), New York, Schocken Books, 1970, pp. 38–40. (NV)

In the pursuit of Truth there is no room for weakness or defeat. Gandhi bore great sufferings for the sake of Truth. For example, 2,338 days in prison, fasting, privations, insults, humiliations, and finally death. He does not seek Truth in a Himalayan cave, but rather in his fellow man in need.

Ahimsa

Ahimsa, not-harming, love, is Gandhi's second vow and the road to Satya. Ahimsa was strong in Hindu tradition from the days of Mahavira and Gautama. It is the other side of Satya, for God is both Love and Truth.

Gandhi loved all men, be they good or evil. When we attack one of our fellow men, we really strike out at ourselves.

> We are all children of one and the same Creator, and as such the divine powers within us are infinite. To slight a single human being is to slight those divine powers, and thus to harm not only that being, but with him the whole world (A 337).

Westerners do not understand the solidarity of all men in Purusha, Atman, Satya, but it is a fundamental teaching of Hinduism.

Ahimsa, Gandhi writes in 1918,[4] "really means that you may not offend anybody; you may not harbor uncharitable thoughts even with one who may consider himself your enemy." If we really love our enemy, he must return our love.

4. *The Gandhi Reader,* ed. H. Jack, Bloomington, Ind., Indiana University Press, 1956, pp. 174–175. (GR)

Though Gandhi is against war, he served in the ambulance corps in the Boer War and supported the British in World War I. How does he square this with ahimsa? Though ahimsa is the ideal, all life involves some himsa. We must stop all war. But what if we cannot? "He who is not qualified to resist war may take part in war, and yet wholeheartedly try to free himself, his nation, and the world from war" (A 428).

Ahimsa includes not only men but animals as well for all are united in the cycle of life. This is the basis of Gandhi's vegetarianism with Jain origins.

Since ahimsa is universal love, self-love must go. "I must reduce myself to zero. So long as a man of his own free will does not put himself last among his fellow creatures, there is no salvation for him. Ahimsa is the farthest limit of humility" (A 615).

Ahimsa is like balancing on the edge of a sword. Without constant striving, one fails. But what about those who attack us? We do not make headway by destroying others. On the other hand, "the man who suffered those who created difficulties marched ahead and at times even took others with him" (NV 40–42). Ahimsa means suffering and patience which lead slowly to truth, peace of mind, and humility.

Ahimsa tells us not to hurt any living thing. But this is the bottom line. "The principle of ahimsa is hurt by every evil thought, by undue haste, by lying, by hatred, by wishing ill to anybody." We violate ahimsa by holding onto something for ourselves which the world needs.

People criticized Gandhi's nonviolent crusade against British injustice as weakness. But ahimsa can tame the wildest beast. And it is a force more positive than electricity.

Under Buddhism, ahimsa civilized some of the wildest tribes of Asia.

"One person who can express ahimsa in life exercises a force superior to all the forces of brutality." Whereas the violent man trains for war with weapons, the man of ahimsa practices love and kindness and self-effacement. In place of armor, he is vulnerable (GR 313-316).

Gandhi felt that the use of the atom bomb by the USA was a gross violation of ahimsa. Whereas ahimsa is soul force, eternal, unchangeable, the atom bomb is physical force and corruptible. Hatred can only be overcome by love.

Brahmacharya

Brahmacharya is Satyagraha. Both mean the pursuit of God in a wholehearted manner and flow from the inclusive love of ahimsa.

Brahmacharya is an ancient Hindu tradition going back to the Upanishads. It is found in the celibate student of the Brahmacharya Ashrama and in the retired sannyasis, the yogis, and the bhikkhus. Gandhi makes it the third vow of his Satyagraha.

In 1906 at the age of 37 with the permission of his wife, Kasturbai, Gandhi took the vow of brahmacharya, becoming a vanaprasthya, dedicating himself totally to the service of his fellow man. (A 254) Far from restricting him, the vow freed him for universal love.

"Now the vow was a sure shield against temptation. The great potential of brahmacharya daily became more patent to me" (A 256-7). But still it is not easy. Strict vegetarian

diet and fasting help control the passions. Also mental
fasting is necessary. "The existence of God within makes
even control of the mind possible" (A 259).
    Gandhi sees total dedication to Satyagraha and exclusive
family life as incompatible.

> A man whose activities are wholly consecrated to the reali-
> zation of truth, which requires utter selflessness, can have
> no time for the selfish purpose of begetting children and
> running a household (NV 42–45).

· Self-realization and self-gratification are not compatible.
    How are ahimsa and brahmacharya related? Ahimsa is
universal love and so not harmonious with the exclusive
love of marriage. "One who would obey the law of ahimsa
cannot marry, not to speak of gratification outside of the
marital bond."
    What if a couple is married? Gandhi lived as brother and
sister with Kasturbai to be free for universal service. Actually their mutual love, freed from lust, grew stronger.
    Brahmacharya means total pursuit of Brahman and so a
leaving behind of the wordly, sensual. The unchaste man
is weak and cowardly. He also opposed artificial birth control for he felt it promoted lust and used women for men's
pleasure.
    He believes in the sublimation of sexuality for Satyag-
raha. This is based on ancient Hindu psychosomatic principles.

> All power comes from the preservation and sublimation of
> the vitality that is responsible for the creation of life. If the
> vitality is husbanded instead of being dissipated, it is trans-
> muted into creative energy of the highest order (GR 306).

Sexual energy can be easily dissipated. But he who con-
serves his power has inner strength for Satyagraha.

Aparigraha

Aparigraha, renunciation, is Gandhi's fourth vow and is
based on the long Hindu tradition of the sannyasis and the
bhikkhus. It complements the first three insofar as one
must give up all illusions (maya) including self, sex, and
possessions in order to seek Satya, Reality, and Truth and
to serve others in Satya. Christian monastic tradition calls
this the vow of poverty.

Gandhi kept no money for himself. All went for Satyagraha. He even had doubts about insurance for his family.
This is the teaching of the bhikkhus, the beggars, who put
away nothing for tomorrow, relying wholly on God. "If,
therefore, we repose faith in his providence, we should
rest assured that he will give us every day our daily bread,
meaning everything that we require" (NV 45-50).

It is the ignorance (avidya) of God's providence that
causes the grave inequities and suffering between rich and
poor. "If each retained possession only of what he needed,
no one would be in want, and all would live in content-
ment."

Perfect aparigraha means complete freedom from
maya. The satyagrahi, as the bhikkhu, has no roof, clothes,
or food for tomorrow. Some of the Jain monks who influ-
enced Gandhi went around naked and fasted exceedingly,
sometimes even to death.

Gandhi used fasting not only to keep his passions in line,

but also by his suffering to bring about Truth, justice, and harmony. It is also ahimsa, for it harms no one else.

Sometimes he fasted to make reparation for the bad karma of others which brought harm to Satyagraha. Since all are one in Satya, when one sins, all are affected. And when one does reparation, others are healed. So when two members of his ashram at Phoenix were immoral, Gandhi fasted seven days total fast and a month and a half partial fast.

His fasting is only a means to Satyagraha. "It will have to come in obedience to the call of Truth, which is God. I will not be a traitor to God to please the whole world" (NV 315).

Fasting from food and other sense pleasures and possessions brings Gandhi into a closer union with Satya. Fasting is really prayer, or a preparation for it. "It is a yearning of the soul to merge in the divine essence." There is no prayer without fasting.

"A complete fast is a complete and literal denial of self. It is the truest prayer. . . . It has to be reckless and joyous giving without the least reservation." Abstention from food and drink is just the beginning of self-immolation (NV 318).

In fasting the body eats itself (autophagous) and in humility the soul eats itself (anatman). What is left? Satya, Being, Reality, Truth, God. But one must have an inner fast before he can attempt an outer one. This is just an irrepressible longing for Truth and it includes love of enemies, freedom from passions and possessions (NV 319).

Are fasts coercive? Yes, insofar as they are tapas, renunciation, purification, heat. Thus Gandhi put the heat on the unjust politicians, diplomats, and wealthy. And so he helped them to be purified and so seek Truth. Fasting can also aid those without food. Overeating is really theft and anthropophagous. If we eat more than our share, the starving have to eat themselves. So, indirectly, we eat them. Aparigraha is renunciation and sharing and this in justice, not merely benevolence. Gandhi felt that charity and justice are one.

Satyagraha

Besides the four main vows of Satyagraha, Gandhi also taught: fearlessness, control of the palate, nonstealing, bread-labor, equality of religions, antiuntouchability and self-rule.

Satyagraha, whether practiced in South Africa against white discrimination, or fighting the Indigo Tax in Bihar, or marching on the Dharasana Salt Works to protest the British Salt Tax, is based on nonviolence, or love. The British were not hated or harmed, only their unjust laws protested because they violated Satya. Though Satyagraha is based on love, it is not weak, for it knows no fear.

All Satyagraha, whether protesting British injustice or child marriage or untouchability, is a seeking after Truth, God.

Is Gandhi a mystic? If a mystic is one who vehemently pursues God, then Gandhi is a mystic. For this is what Satyagraha and Brahmacharya are all about. But he does not flee to a cave high in the Himalayas to seek moksha or nirvana through jnana or sacred wisdom, but rather takes the margas of karma and bhakti, action and devotion.

For Gandhi, Satya, Brahman is in other people, especially the poor, lowly untouchables who possess little maya and so live closer to Satya. Gandhi emulated their way of life. Winston Churchill laughed at his dhoti. But his humility won many and he is called the Father of India. The people named him Mahatma, the Great-Souled One, united to the universal soul, Atman, and so one with all other men: rich, poor, maharajas, untouchables, British, Hindus, Moslems, Christians. So by his prayer, fasting, suffering renunciation and chastity he can lift up all to Satya.

IV

SIMONE WEIL
Malheur De Dieu

Simone Weil, French philosopher and mystic, also absorbed much from Hindu traditions of spirituality. In fact, the Bhagavad Gita was her favorite reading. Simone had a remarkable intellect and memory and synthesized the best of Eastern, Western, classical, and modern thought into a philosophia or theologia perennis. She grew up in the interbella period that produced Sartre, Marcel, DeBeauvoir, and others.

Even as a little girl, Simone was concerned with suffering, offering her food for the hungry prisoners of World War I. Her own life was filled with suffering: frequent migraine or sinus headaches, pleurisy, weak stomach, and fatigue.

Although a teacher by profession, she was well aware of the suffering working classes, taking an active part in union meetings and laboring at the Renault plant in Paris to feel the pain and frustration of being daily fastened to a machine.

In 1936 she volunteered for the Popular Front in the Spanish Civil War. But she had no illusions about Communism, seeing little difference between the totalitarianism of Russia and Germany.

Gradually Simone, though of Jewish parentage, was drawn to Christianity. As the Nazis took over France, she

was forbidden to teach because of her race. She went with
her family to the USA, but did not stay long for she wanted
to return to suffer with her people. Working for De Gaulle
in England, she was refused permission to parachute into
France. But she minimized her diet to correspond to the
poor fare of her countrymen.

Malheur De Dieu

Probably Weil's greatest contributions to twentieth century thought are her essays on suffering. Her own life was
austere, eating little, sleeping on the hard floor. "Fix your
attack on it and suffer from it."[1] She does not pray for
relief from her headaches and her resignation to her long
term affliction brings her to a state of exhaustion.

Suffering is the indispensable way from time to eternity
(N 213). But all suffering that is not detached is wasted
and leaves us cold and warped (N 216). We must not flee
the incarnation and its suffering by living in imagination.
Imagination disincarnates and is from Satan (N 218).

Suffering should not just test our physical endurance.
Rather it is a testimony of human misery to be endured
passively. This is the door leading to wisdom and eternal
life (N 236).

Long-enduring suffering takes away time's orientation
so that one passes from time into eternity. Affliction,
long-enduring, tries to hold onto anything for support.
But to accept death is total detachment.

Suffering is where the finite meets the infinite. So man
must suffer when he is united to the supernatural. And we

1. Simone Weil, *Notebooks*, New York, Putnam's Sons, 1956, p. 128.
(N)

must empty ourselves of all imaginary consolations to make room for God (N 228).

But affliction seems so unjust. However, on those in a state of supernatural love affliction can have no effect. It can only bother those whose souls are at the level of evil (N 273).

By seeing affliction as human misery and not just the suffering of an isolated individual, one sees God captive in the flesh. "And at that instant every man acquires a fellow-likeness to Christ." So our contemplation of human misery can pull us towards God (N 281).

If there were no affliction in this world we might think ourselves already in paradise. And we should neither seek out affliction, nor avoid it so that when it comes it will be pure and bitter (N 294).

Is suffering evil? Not if I do not think it evil for me. Thus one can willingly accept suffering for himself and feel compassion for others. Evil is the distance between God and man begun in creation. And it is abolished through decreation (N 342).

"To pathei mathos." It is necessary to suffer in order to receive wisdom and impart it (N 413). Bitter agony is the dark night of the soul and even helps the perfect attain absolute purity. Then pure joy causes the soul to burst with the happiness of God's presence (N 467-8).

Suffering is a koan, Zen meditation puzzle, supplied to the soul by God—indigestible, contradictory, irrational, unfathomable. Here discursive knowledge is useless, for only intuition can perceive. To regard suffering as an offering or as a punishment is to obscure it. "Suffering has no significance.... We must love it in its reality, which is the absence of significance. Otherwise we do not love God" (N 483-4).

Simone never asked God to relieve her fatigue for this would seem to go against God's tender love which had given her the precious gift of affliction.[2]

Affliction differs from simple suffering insofar as it marks the soul as a slave. Long term physical suffering is affliction.

> Affliction is an uprooting of life, a more or less attenuated equivalent of death, made irresistibly present to the soul by the attack and immediate apprehension of physical pain (W 117).

Extreme affliction is like a nail whose point is at the center of the soul and whose broad head is necessity spreading through time and space. It is God's technique introducing into the soul the immensity of a finite blind brutal and cold force. The infinite distance between God and man is concentrated into one point, piercing the soul at its center (W 135).

Though man is pinned by God, the acquiescent part of his soul remains consenting in the right direction. Although the nail pierces his soul, he remains turned towards God and is nailed to the center of the universe, at the intersection of Creator and creation, God on the cross.

Affliction is imposed so harshly that there is no opportunity for lying about it. Though not evil, it wounds deeply and degrades (W 207).

Force, such as the Nazi occupation of France, is a great source of affliction.[3] Force turns man into a stone, a thing, a corpse. Force and violence degrade both the employer

---

2. Simone Weil, *Waiting for God,* New York, Harper and Row, 1973, p. 100. (W)

3. Simone Weil, *The Iliad,* Poem of Force, Wallingford, PA, Pendle Hill, 1957, p. 19. (I)

and his victim (I 19). So the conquering soldier also becomes a thing. Submission to force is really submission to matter. "Only he who has measured the dominion of force, and knows how to respect it, is capable of love and justice"(I 34).

It is to lead man to supreme purity that God allows him to cross the whole expanse of suffering and darkness, abandoned and alone.[4]

Whereas creation (gravity) draws us away from God, God uses suffering as a decreation to pull us towards him. It is too bad that some who go down the road of pain, after a certain period reach their limit and become debased (G 8).

Some place all their hopes in the future and then become disillusioned when the future becomes present. Only eternity can keep the future as future and present (G 18).

We should not so much seek to escape our suffering or to mitigate it, as to remain untainted by it. Thus Christianity does not seek a spiritual remedy for suffering, but rather a supernatural use of it (G 73).

The virtue of patience does not change suffering into crime, but vice versa (G 66). Whereas the false god changes suffering into violence, the true god turns violence into suffering. Crime passes evil and degradation onto others, but Christ turns evil into his own suffering (G 65).

The better we feel the fullness of joy, the more pure and intense will be our suffering in affliction and our compassion for the afflicted. But suffering takes away nothing from him who is without joy (G 76).

Why? This is the big question of suffering. Why me? But to explain suffering is to console it, therefore, it must not

4. Simone Weil, *Gravity and Grace*, London, Routledge, 1974, p. xxxii. (G)

be explained. When we ask God: Why? he is silent. "Whatever I may have to bear, when God sends me suffering, I am inescapably forced to suffer all that there is to suffer" (G 114).

Though pain keeps us nailed to time, the acceptance of pain carries us into eternity. Pain, fatigue, hunger, exhaustion give time the color of eternity.[5] "Every contact between God and man is pain on both sides" (F 211).

In pain a small part of the soul consents that this should continue through all time, if God so wishes (F 218). When one's animal energy wanes, leaving only vegetal vim, after only fifteen minutes, the part of the soul that refuses to give in, travels the whole length of time into eternity (F 220).

The soul tends to flee both God and affliction. "The only soul that can fix its attention on affliction is one that has been killed by a true contact with the true God" (F 327). One can only feel the bitterness of affliction at the very center of his soul by imitating Job who still loved God in the midst of his affliction.

Gravity and Void

While gravity and creation pull us down, grace and decreation raise us up. Thus those condemned to death lower their heads. Imaginary affliction carries with it no gravity, so it is hard for a spectator to feel sympathy with the afflicted.

Ingratitude produces a void in the benefactor. But when the void is not accepted, it gives off hate, bitterness, and

5. Simone Weil, *First and Last Notebooks*, London, Oxford University Press, 1970, p. 208. (F)

malice and the transfer of evil to the one who hates (N 139).

Acceptance of the void may take many forms. For example, hunger and thirst can be hunger and thirst for God. Abraham's sacrifice would be another instance (N 137). The void leads to anguish, exhaustion, and resignation with a loss of a sense of reality. Acceptance of the void makes lying unnecessary. But the imagination can fill the void. Thus one can suffer all sorts of degradation: slavery, prison, torture without purification (N 145).

When those who cause us suffering are safely out of reach (usually the case) and those who are good to us are near, smiles through the pain. The void (N 147). People expect the smiles (gravity), and if they do not get them it creates a void in them. "The void is when there is nothing external to correspond to an internal tension" (N 147).

The void should be eliminated from society as much as possible for it is only useful in the life of grace (N 148).

Faithfulness to Christ is difficult in the void. Deus absconditus. We should set aside all beliefs that tend to soften the void, such as immortality and the usefulness of sins. Sins are really just man's futile attempts to fill the void.

"My life with all its stains is close to his perfectly pure one," for Christ suffered the void, all those things that make us capable of sin.

When one reaches the end of his rope so that he can no longer bear it, he feels the void. "It accompanies all true suffering and breaks through as soon as the imagination ceases to fill the void" (N 153). The imagination is a liar. One should never seek or try to avoid the void.

Somebody slights me and so creates a void. When life

seems sweet at the precise moment when it is not preferable to death—void.

To accept suffering is to accept the void. And to renounce rewards is to live in the void (N 227). We try to fill
the void with past memories and future hopes. We fly
from the void because God might be in it.

Innocent Suffering and the Cross

Only innocent suffering can redeem. "Everyone who
does not take up the sword will perish by the cross" (N
229). The innocent one bears the whole weight of the universe. Suffering is absolute, exterior, and essential to the
innocent (N 230).

Blood on the snow. Innocence and evil. When the innocent one suffers, he sheds the light of salvation on evil. He
reflects the innocent God. "That is why a god who loves
man and a man who loves God must suffer" (N 234).

Redemptive suffering is when a man has completely reduced his "I." It is the plenitude of the cross and the absence of God. Through redemptive suffering God is present in extreme evil through his absence (N 343). Moreover, he needs man's cooperation to travel to the end of
creation, the extremity of evil.

Redemption is the focal point of the passion. Christ in
the absolute purity of his (finite) soul—a purity that implies extreme suffering—redeems the world, and redemption continues in those who imitate Christ (N 383).

The pure being transforms sin into suffering. All the
evil in the Roman empire became suffering in the innocent
Christ. Evil people, however, turn suffering into sin. Redemptive suffering brings about the absence of God in a
soul emptied of self through love (G 24).

Evil is passed down until it hits a pure innocent being who suffers it and destroys it. "It is only God in this world, having become a victim, who can destroy evil by suffering it."[6] Man sacrifices innocent victims for the purification of his sin. For example, animals, children, or virgins. Purity attracts evil which rushes toward it as a moth to a flame to be consumed (W 218).

When pain and exhaustion give the feeling of perpetuity in the soul and we are caught up in eternity—the cross (N 282).

The agony of the cross consisted in gravity. (Prometheus and Atlas) The crucified body is in perfect balance, reduced to its point in time and space (N 214).

Crucifixion and human destiny. "How could a being whose essence it is to love God and who finds himself situated in space and time have any other vocation than the cross?" (N 268). Simone asks God that time enter into her soul like a cross, the nails of the cross (N 271).

One should uproot himself from home, social, and vegetative life, cut the tree down and make a cross of it and carry it always (N 298).

In the passion of creation the soul of the world is crucified between the fixed stars and the sun, fastened to the cross of time. The lamb is slain from the beginning (N 380).

The idea of justice is to be naked and dead without any imagination. The cross is not open to imaginary imitation. To show the distance between him and us, God became a crucified slave (N 411).

We do not become like God by eating the fruit of the tree as Adam did, but by hanging from it as the Second

6. Simone Weil, *Waiting for God*, New York, Harper and Row, 1973, p. 153. (W)

Adam. Though we cannot desire the cross, by contemplating our wretchedness in Christ, we can learn to love it (N 414).

"The absolutely pure desire for the greatest possible amount of good implies the acceptance for oneself of the last degree of affliction—of the cross" (N 414).

One cannot desire the cross for it is a penal form of suffering and therein lies its contradiction. For it is a free will offering and at the same time a punishment against one's will. So the cross is infinitely greater than martyrdom. The irreducible nature of suffering arrests the will. Man comes to the end of his faculties, stretches out his arms, stops, looks up, and waits for the cross (N 415).

The cross is a fulcrum on which the frail body of God was able to lift the whole world at the point of intersection of the world and the nonworld, time and eternity.

"Pain, by forcing us to associate ourselves with God's harmonizing action, alone repairs sin which has separated us from God.... To love pain means associating oneself with the unity—transcendent with respect to ourselves—of the power and love of God" (N 539).

Hang a man on a tree. Gravity pulls him down while solar energy in the tree sustains him. Descending and ascending, the balance of the cross. Heaven, descending to earth, lifts earth to heaven (N 544).

We have the crucifixion of the God eternal daily in the eucharist. "If, in the communion, the suffering of God is joy to us, must we not think that our suffering, when it is fully consented to, is joy in God?" But we have to consent to its complete bitterness (N 564).

In a sense, man's suffering makes him superior to God. But the incarnation is the great equalizer. Although she could not desire crucifixion for herself, Simone writes,

"Every time I think of the crucifixion of Christ I commit the sin of envy" (W 30). The good thief is her ideal, hanging naked alongside the suffering Jesus (W 59).

By his resurrection Jesus pardons those who killed him. So Easter joy soars above the pain and perfects it (F 69). One should not try to console the afflicted by talking about the kingdom. But only about the cross. Since God suffered, suffering is a divine thing. No compensation or consolation should be sought, but the horrible suffering itself will bear fruit in attentive patience (en hypomene) (F 82).

The suffering line of time stretches through creation, incarnation, and passion, between the Father and the Son. And we are privileged to take part in this distance which the Holy Spirit travels. My misery, even my sins, make me a recipient of the Holy Spirit. "It is in the deepest faith of my misery that I touch God" (F 83).

The supreme mediation is the harmony between Christ's "Why?" which is repeated in every afflicted soul and the Father's silence. The very universe, including us, vibrates with this harmony (F 91).

To accept God crucified as a common criminal is to overcome the world (F 144). Death is the intersection of time and eternity, where the arms of the cross meet (F 177).

Evil cannot do any harm to the good, only to the mediocre. So the cross injures the impenitent thief, but not the good thief or Christ (F 337). The silence of Christ under blows and mockery is the silence of truth and affliction in the world (F 341).

If the tree of life is in man's soul when affliction strikes—he is nailed to the same cross as Christ. Otherwise he must choose between crosses on either side of Christ.

To say like the good thief, "I deserve this crucifixion."[7]
    Though we are weak, we can still share Christ's cross.
"This weakness makes possible in certain conditions, the
operation by which we are nailed to the very center of the
cross" (GT 88). If this is an habitual disposition, then after
a while the cross of Christ should become the very substance of our life.
    "Wherever there is affliction in any age or country, the
cross of Christ is the truth of it." One can only have a part
of the cross if he faces affliction rather than escapes it.
"Only one thing enables us to accept affliction and that is
the contemplation of Christ's cross" (GT 99).

Compassion and the Love of Man

    Loving the neighbor means reading in all the same
natural and supernatural vocation. This is supernatural
reading and goes against gravity. "To love one's neighbor
as oneself is nothing else than to contemplate human misery in oneself and in others" (N 282). Our neighbor is a
mirror for us.
    Compassion for the cold and hungry presupposes the
ability to place oneself in any sort of circumstances, for
example, to be naked. There can be no compassion without recognizing ourselves in the misery of others. Humility
is placing our own "I" in the miserable body before us. It is
a type of incarnation in which we empty ourselves of false
divinity.
    Necessity enables us to suffer while accepting suffering.
"And to transfer through the mind one's own 'self' into

7. Simone Weil, *Gateway to God*, ed., D. Raper, Glasgow, Collins,
1974, p. 87. (GT)

some unhappy being." One must empty himself of false divinity and submit himself unconditionally to the irreducible bitterness of human misery (N 284-5). Could God have compassion on us if he had not been crucified?

By seeing misery in the individual, one reads the spirit captive in the flesh. This is the image of God captive in the flesh. Then one acquires the image of Christ (N 281). By contemplating human misery in others, loved as ourselves, we are drawn to God (N 281).

We should not love our neighbor for Christ, but through him. When our "I" disappears, Christ himself goes to help the neighbor. We are the servant whom the master sends to assist others (N 358). We are impelled towards our neighbor as an arrow towards a target. We are the point of contact between God and the neighbor as my pen or pencil contacts the paper when I write (N 360).

For pure love of creation my love must pass through God as through a fire. First it detaches itself from creatures and goes to God and then descends from God filled with the creative love of God. And so the two opposites which split love are united. "Loving the loved one just as he is, and desiring to create him anew" (N 616).

Justice means equality where two wills coincide, the stronger coming to the level of the weaker. Gratitude and compassion, the acceptance of affliction both by the afflicted one and his rescuer.

Love of neighbor is creative attention which means giving attention to that which does not exist, for example, the poor and slaves or prisoners. "Love sees what is invisible" (N 149). Only God in us can read a human quality into these neglected victims.

Love of neighbor is really God's love for man, for he is present when our eyes meet the eyes of the afflicted.

Almsgiving and punishment without charity are really forms of prostitution, treating people as things (N 156).

Friendship, pure personal and human love, can also reflect divine love. But charity is not exclusive or discriminating. If it is more abundant in one place, it is because affliction is there. But affliction can come to all and so is not exclusive (W 200).

Friendship is a sacrament, imitating the friendship of God. When two meet, respecting the distance between them, God is present in each. Parallel lines meet at infinity (W 208).

"To love a stranger as oneself implies the reverse: to love oneself as a stranger" (G 55). Love of the happy one means wishing to share the suffering of his unhappy beloved.

Justice demands that we admit that another person is something quite different from what we read. "Everything cries out to be read differently." What hope is there for innocence if it is not recognized? We should never judge others, for even Christ does not judge us. Rather he is our judgment. "Suffering innocence is the measure" (G 123).

Mercy means coming down from what is not suffering to what is suffering, as the silent compassion of the Father for the Son. Part of the soul suffers and part is with the Father. Dialogue: Christ's cry and the Father's silence. Compassion means that the spiritual part of our soul is with God while the carnal part is naked, as Christ hung bare on the cross (F 94–5).

Christ recognizes as his benefactors those whose compassion rests in the knowledge of affliction. Others are patronizing. There can be no distance between myself and the other, projecting my own being into him and giving him a new personality.

In affliction we are stripped away, slipping into anonymity, as Christ empties himself. "The man who sees someone in affliction and projects into him his own being, brings to birth in him through love, at least for a moment, an existence apart from affliction." To assume another's affliction, only Christ and those whose whole soul he possesses can do it.

Charity is like a sacrament, "a supernatural process by which a man in whom Christ dwells really puts Christ into the soul of the afflicted." If bread is given—the host! "If you do it to one of these, you do it to me." Therefore, Christ is naked, hungry, in prison, etc. He is present in each act of charity. "Who could be Christ's benefactor except Christ himself" (F 94–5).

Compassion loves all equally as the sun. Contempt for crime and admiration for greatness are balanced by compassion. "Every movement of pure compassion in a soul is a new descent of Christ upon earth to be crucified" (F 97). Compassion is parallel to creation, and so it cannot exclude a single creature. It spans the abyss between God and creation (F 103).

Compassion is the recognition of one's own misery in someone else (F 209). Love means loving created beings as the divine Word loved them when he emptied himself to become a slave, and loving God as he did on the cross (F 274).

We must love in men either their desire or their possession of God unconditionally, to love human beings in God (F 284). Loving our neighbor's hunger implies that we stop feeding on man and want to feed on God (F 286).

The compassionate man does not run away from affliction, for he knows that it is not evil. Rather he suffers at its pain which impels him to try to remedy it (F 318). And his compassion shows he is united to God by love.

Humility and Renunciation

Perhaps Simone Weil's most noted virtue is her humility—unobtrusive, waiting patiently for her spiritual guide, Fr. Perrin, not wanting to be a bother, not wanting to be an obstacle between God and God, between God's love of himself in another, killing her "ego."

After renunciation of material and spiritual goods, what is left? Nothing! Spiritual nakedness! Humility is to be assimilated to God. I must take away from myself all that I am. There remains—humility, moral gravity, making us fall to the heights.

To feel the wretchedness of Christ is sainthood. This is to endure suffering without alleviation, hunger without food, and humiliation without honor (N 128).

Renunciation is a passing through anguish equivalent to that caused by the loss of all: loved ones, possessions, faculties, opinions, etc. But the anguish should not be broken up and spread out or alleviated by a future hope.

In order to be detached one must pass through irreducible pain, as Job, and Christ on the cross, affliction without consolation. Self-emptying means reducing to the point one occupies in time and space, to become nothing (N 212). Absolute solitude, truth.

The humble man believes himself to be below others in order to be equal and not superior. "By dint of maintaining oneself on the lowest rung, the ladder disappears" (N 239).

To love human misery is to be happy that one is nothing

(N 274). "Humiliations turn away from the path of humility those in whom there is not already at any rate a beginning of supernatural love." Humility is the knowledge that one is nothing. Decreation.

Simone's prayer. "O God, grant that I may become nothing. As fast as I become nothing, God loves himself through me" (N 292). We must become nothing right down to the vegetal level. Then God becomes bread.

God cannot be close at hand without his proximity destroying the "I." "We must reply to the absence of God by our own absence and love" (N 403–4). The "I" is just the shadow of sin and error which obscures God's light (N 419).

I am nothing. Perhaps God likes rejects such as the stone thrown away by the builders. Even if bread is moldy, it still can become the body of Christ (W 72).

Through love God consented to cease to be everything so that we could be something. We must become nothing so that God can once again be everything. Killing the "I" by exposing it naked to the wounds of life. The self is destroyed within by love and without by suffering and degradation (G xxi). The hero wears armor to protect him from affliction, whereas the saint is naked.

To teach us that we should be nothing, God made himself nothing. If we destroy our "I" from within, affliction can no longer destroy it from without.

When our ego is elevated, we confuse ourselves with it. But when it is debased, we know we are not that. Just as an ugly person looks in the mirror and knows that he is not what he sees (G 29).

Every day God makes himself matter to be consumed by us. So man through fatigue, affliction, etc. is made matter and consumed by God.

Humility destroys the imagination. The real is hard and rough. The pleasant belongs to dreams. Man flees his painful incarnation to his imagination and its false divinity.

The chief use of suffering is to teach us that we are nothing. We must love God through our suffering, and love being nothing. God gives grace to the individual insofar as he ceases to be an individual (G 101).

Humility is the root of love, and so has irresistible power over God. If God had not been humiliated in Christ, he would be inferior to us. Humility gives us power over God because we resemble his Son. But this calls for a completely humbled and broken heart, waiting in silence, as a slave for his master, transmuting time into eternity (F 99).

While pride of the flesh gives us a certain hold on the future, privation proves our impotence. Humility tells us that the future is not me. "The transcendent bread is the bread of today. Therefore, it is the food of a humble soul" (F 102).

To say "I" is a lie. Lord, I am nothing except error and error is nothing (F 132). Humility is inevitable when I am unsure of the future.

Humility is to be a child, horizontal before one can be vertical. The seed must die before it can rise. So we should be buried in renunciation and silence before we can ascend (F 262).

Simone Weil died at age 34 on August 24, 1943, exiled from country, family, and friends, in a sanatorium in Ashford, Kent, England. Frustrated in her wishes to return to France to help her people, weakened by a life of ill health, tuberculosis, fatigue, and bad appetite, and a feeling that her life had been useless, she was ready for her total renunciation.

But her sometimes sketchy and disconnected pensées,

penetrating the sham and artificiality of life to the Truth, would live on.

Though never formally baptized with water, Simone had accepted joyfully the cross of Christ and borne it uncomplaining through her life. "Affliction, when it is consented to, accepted, and loved, is truly a baptism."

V

MARGUERITE-MARIE AND PIERRE TEILHARD DE CHARDIN
The Spiritual Energy of Suffering

Pierre Teilhard de Chardin, Jesuit anthropologist and paleontologist, is another outstanding intellect of the French interbella period. His sister, Marguerite-Marie, though not well known, had a great influence on his life, especially in the value of suffering in God's plan for the universe.

War Writings

As a young priest stretcher-bearer in the medical corps during World War I, Pierre witnessed suffering at its insanest. Two of his brothers were killed in the conflict. The painful carnage inspired a number of essays on suffering and death which laid the foundations for his later works such as the *Divine Milieu*.

A firm believer in evolution, Pierre sought the place of suffering in the progress of the universe. In his *Cosmic Life*[1] (4/24/16) he outlines four stages of man's spiritual evolution: the mastery of the universe, the segregation of

1. *Writings in Time of War*, tr. R. Hague, New York, Harper and Row, 1967.

man, the liberation of the spirit, and the peace that the world gives and the soul's lament.

In stage three, as his consciousness as a person grows, man sees matter as an obstacle: dim, heavy, passive, suffering, evil. Either it must be spiritualized or eliminated.

In the final harmony, "suffering and mischance and gloom will no longer disfigure the regenerated cosmos" (41). All hardness, falsity, physical and moral evil will disappear and what remains will reflower and matter will be absorbed by spirit.

In the fourth stage, man has that peace that the world gives. Searching for the absolute, his ego drops and he feels others' needs. Now he sees his suffering as an important part of cosmic evolution.

> Observed in isolation, pain is inexplicable and hateful. But as soon as we attribute to it its proper place and role in the cosmos, we can read its features and distinguish its smile (43).

Pain wakes us up and turns us away from ways that hinder our full development. Pain detaches us from lower delights and helps us to seek our happiness in things that endure. Pain expiates life's errors, it spiritualizes and purifies man, and it complements our appetite for pleasure.

"It is the very life blood of evolution. Since, through suffering, it is the cosmos that wakes us up, I shall see suffering come without distress and fear" (43).

The soul is discouraged over frustrated hopes. Little that we do lasts. We make mistakes, have breakdowns. Our efforts seem useless and our sufferings barren.

In a way, failure can be preferable to success, since it

offers us a wider basis of sanctification. Christ established the primacy of humility and suffering.

> The road along which his kingdom makes progress is the way of relinquishment. of blood and tears—the way of the cross. It is thus, as though through a painful metamorphosis—a whole life being born from a whole death—that the divine cosmos germinates from the ruins of the old earth (53).

We are caught between heaven's design and the earth's ambition. But the cross is the victory of duty over attraction, spirit over senses, good over evil. We must resign ourselves to not being made use of, to be useless and ineffective. Hosts of failures are the price of success. "The obscure, the useless, the failures, should take joy in the superiority of the others whose triumph they lend support to and pay for" (67).

We hope that suffering and evil are transitory and will be eliminated by advances in science and culture. However, the more subtle and complex man becomes, the higher are the chances of disorder and greater gravity. We cannot build up a mountain without first digging a pit. "Everything that becomes, suffers and sins. The truth about our position in this world is that we are on a cross" (67).

Christ on the cross is the focal point of all earthly sufferings and the place where they are healed. God gathers up all our sufferings to himself. We can appreciate the immensity of Christ's suffering when we see in it, "An anguish that reflects every anguish ever experienced, a 'cosmic suffering'" (67). Christ bears in his soul, alone and forsaken, the heavy burden of human sorrows and he transfigures them.

Without Christ, suffering and sin would become the earth's "slag-heap." Useless labor, failure, frustrated effort. But the cross makes all this a storehouse of treasure. "There is a wonderful compensation by which physical evil, if humbly accepted, conquers moral evil" (68). It purifies the soul, spurs it, and detaches it.

Suffering is a sacrament, a mysterious union between the faithful soul and the suffering Christ. If it is pursued in surrender and in a spirit of conquest, "The pursuit of Christ in the world culminates logically in an impassioned enfolding, heavy with sorrow, in the arms of the cross" (68).

When the soul reaches the end of its suffering, it knows that its most effective and peaceful work is to gather together the sufferings of the world and to soothe them and offer them to God. A cosmic compassion.

In cosmic life suffering is the consequence of the work of development and the price of it. The very process of becoming produces physical and moral evil. Everything that evolves has its own sufferings and commits its own faults.

In his "Struggles Against the Multitude" (1917)[2] Teilhard seems almost Hindu when he calls multiplicity the source of suffering. When the one became two, suffering was born.

Pain is the perception of our diminution of being, the insufficiently reduced multitude within. "If complete dissociation could be felt, it would, by annihilating us, produce absolute suffering" (98).

It is painful to live through stages that separate plurality from unity. A divine spur pulls away from multiplicity

2. *Writings in Time of War*, pp. 93–114.

towards simplicity and beatification. From without there is
a multitude of fragmentation, violence and contagion and
within—badly disciplined lives.

The battle rages "at the borderline of body and soul, in
that region of slow release in which spirit emerges from
flesh" (99).

Our simplicity is dragged into fragmentation in every
direction, leaving us with painful scars, a restless plurality
in our unity, at the heart of our spirituality. Antagonisms
and discords come to the surface, tormenting us, as if parts
of our soul were tearing off.

Our personal interior multitude with its many conflicts
and passions and the universal multitude outside. "The
suffering of being a wandering fragment of an unfinished
whole." Our soul is lonely in the throng. Exhausted, we
think we hear our own little self-centered being calling for
happiness. But it is the groaning of the universal soul
weeping for its multitude and yearning for total union
(101).

We are weary of banging against the walls of our opaque
body, of not finding the answer in sensible things, or the
way that leads from one soul to another.

We have within us the pain of individuation. "It is a
ceaseless vibration deep within us, of which our individual
agonies and raptures are passing harmonies" (102).

Our suffering and longing are a summons calling us to a
more perfect unity. "Why should we persist in aggravating
by our own fault and doubling by sin, the pain of the
multitude?"

Sin is a misguided try for unity. The flesh tells us that
the spirit is following the wrong path. So we give up and
fling ourselves on the multitude as our bride.

The concupiscence of the mind hopes to overcome the fragmentation of beings by reducing them to its own unity in pride and egotism. Pride and selfishness degrade the world and keep it chained to materiality (103).

When the immortal soul appeared, it created a crisis of individuation, and a counterattack by the suffering, guilty multitude. But our temporary disintegration is ordered to a more perfect reconstruction of the spirit through incarnation (107).

Purity in the individual and charity in society are not just a lessening of suffering or a soothing of the wounds of society, rather the world is spiritualized.

As Christ becomes incarnate in the universe and expels the guilty plurality. "Step by step, the evil effect of the multitude—suffering—retreats and decreases" (110).

Pain is still with us. But in our ravaged flesh and tormented soul we are molded for eternal life.

Christ comes to fill our void. Our passions are subdued and our flesh acquiescent to the spirit. Lonely souls communicate through Christ.

"Christ gathers up for the life of tomorrow our stifled ambitions, our inadequate understandings, our uncompleted and clumsy, but sincere endeavors . . ." (111).

We have to depersonalize ourselves in order to become centered on Christ. If happiness lies in unification, simplification lies in suffering. "The same pain that kills and decomposes is essential to being if it is to live and become spirit."

Our soul has parasitic branches that reach out for evil and useless pleasures. So man needs to be purified before he can join God. To be one and blessed, "the soul must first be divided. It must suffer a sort of decomposition, and carry within itself the pain of the multitude." Our inner unity must be diminished if we are to be born again in Christ. The grain of wheat must die before it can rise. In his "Mystical Milieu" (8/13/17)[3] Teilhard notes the sensitivity of the mystic to suffering. The mystic searches for the absolute in disintegrating creation. Teilhard himself would suffer exiles, misunderstandings, and painful and probably jealous restrictions on his writings from the officials of his own order.

One must painfully plunge into multiplicity if he is to experience the rapture that transports the soul upwards to enduring Reality (124).

The beautiful flower withers, the wall blocks, and paper burns. But there is no unalleviated sadness, no frustration at the uncertainties and limitation of creation. Rather joy in disappointments and the collapse of earthly supports. You alone are stable (126-7)! It is through sorrow that the Godhead gradually assumes the higher reality in our senses. Someday everything temporal will collapse. Then his naked form will rise up from the ruins.

> What is there in suffering that commits me so deeply to you? Why, when you stretched out nets to imprison me should I have thrilled with greater joy than when you offered me wings (131)?

As a boat sails easily before the wind, one does not feel God's influence when all goes well. But if a sudden squall blows up, then he senses the Lord's strength behind him.

The disappointments and chains of life are blessed. "Blessed . . . the inexorable bondage of time that goes too slowly and frets our impatience, of time that goes too

3. *Writings in Time of War*, pp. 124-144.

quickly and ages us, of time that never stops and never returns." Blessed be death and the horror of falling back into cosmic forces (131).

The value of sorrow lies in its involuntariness. "In nobis sine nobis." If pain is not something forced on us against our will, its heavenly aura disappears and we flee in disgust (132). But it is normal to fight against pain even though it is sent by God. And the more alive the patient is and dedicated to the divine milieu, the more reluctantly he accepts suffering. But then he takes her as his bride.

God's fire comes down on the mystic as on a burnt offering. So he ceases to be only himself, but a fragment of the divine and God passes through him. One may think that a mystic is passive when he sees him immobile or rapt in prayer. But "suffering is dissolving his being, drop by drop, and replacing it by God." Though loving life, he desires death, the destruction of his ego and absorbtion in Christ (144).

As a priest in the midst of war, Teilhard felt himself offering the whole suffering universe as a host to God.[4] The seething cauldron of misery, "Is not that the bitter cup that you seek to sanctify?"

Through the priest the power of the Word comes down on the world to cover its nothingness, wickedness, futility, and disorder. The figure of Christ emerges, but it is Christ crucified.

The wheat is crushed, the dough kneaded and the bread broken before it can be consecrated. "Who shall describe, Lord, the violence suffered by the universe from the moment it falls under your sovereign power?" (209).

Christ is a sword that cuts away the body's useless and

4. "The Priest," *Writings in Time of War,* pp. 204-224.

decayed members. He is the life that brings death to our egoism, drawing to himself our capacity to love.

The universe is rent painfully at its heart as the flesh of Christ is born and grows. As the creation, so the incarnation is achieved in blood. May the blood of Christ, the blood of endeavor and renunciation, mingle with the pain of the world (209). The universe becomes the body and blood of Christ through the consecration of the bread and wine.

Christ is the boundless abyss in which we can relax from our woes. "By growing less in Christo Jesu, those who mortify themselves, who suffer, and grow old with patience cross the critical threshhold at which death is turned into life." We must assist Christ's action through us to the cosmos by offering ourselves to the passivities of life.

Those who suffer and mourn may make their lives useful by allowing God to grow in them and in death to substitute himself for them. So much joy and suffering in the world lies unused. But it can be salvaged in a spirit of self-denial.

Teilhard exhorts his fellow priests serving on the front in World War I "to consecrate into the flesh and blood of Christ the sufferings you see on all sides, and in which your priestly character makes it your duty to share" (233). Priests are God's leaven on the battlefield so that by their presence, "the huge mass of our toil and agony may be transformed." The priest chooses "to be in communion even unto death with the Christ who is being born and suffering in the human race" (224).

Divinization of Passivities

In his *Divine Milieu* (1926)[5] Teilhard notes that the passivities of life comprise about half of our total existence. These are the things that we do not do, but rather undergo. Although we prefer the active side of life, the passive is much wider and deeper.

The passivities of life consistently block our efforts. We can control things only in a limited area of our lives. Beyond this is darkness. But God will enlighten us.

Can any happiness come out of our negative side? For example, how can we find God in death? We suffer diminishments within and without: external obstacles, frustrations, disease, accidents, shocks, severances, death. However, external things we can get back. "What is terrible for us is to be cut off from things through some inward diminishment that cannot be retrieved" (60).

All our diminishments merge in death which we should overcome by finding God in it. By Christ's resurrection nothing kills irrevocably. Thus we can reorder our distraught lives on God (61).

In God's plan for the world there must be diminishments before the final victory, as a soldier dies for a lasting victory and peace. "God does not, therefore, suffer a preliminary defeat because although we appear to succumb individually, the world in which we shall live again triumphs in and through our deaths" (65).

The world is still partially disorganized and on its way to consummation when all diminishments will cease. God transfigures our failures into a better plan. But how can God draw good out of evil? Our material frustrations can

5. London, Collins, 1961, pp. 51ff.

turn us to spiritual goals. As the farmer uses his pruning knife, so we can canalize our vital energies higher.

But how about irredeemable diminishments? For example, child death, accidents, and the like. Man seems permanently diminished. How can these be good? God uses our sufferings to mold us and he makes our losses into points of contact with himself. We have to die to ourselves in order to be united to him. Our mini-deaths are but foretastes of the final moment when we will leap out of ourselves and into his arms.

We cannot win our fight against death. But Christ can win it, transforming death into life. "God must . . . make room for himself, hollowing us out and emptying us, if he is finally to penetrate into us" (68). He has to break us in order to remold us. Death completes our self-emptying. "What was by nature empty and void, a return to bits and pieces, can, in any human existence, become fullness and unity in God" (69).

Communion through diminishment. "Grant . . . that I may recognize you under the species of each alien or hostile force that seems bent upon destroying or uprooting me" (69). Old age, illness, losing hold. "You who are painfully parting the fibres of my being in order to penetrate to the very marrow of my substance and bear me away within yourself." By losing myself and being assimilated into Christ, my death is a communion.

But resignation is not pure passivity. The Christian must fight evil, as God does. Even when defeat inevitably comes, he will still resist inwardly, accepting suffering in faith, though still struggling against it. A human failure, but a divine success.

Christ assumes our sufferings, showing us the way of the cross to the peaks. So life is no longer sad and ugly. "By the virtue of your suffering incarnation disclose to us, and then teach us to harness jealously for you the spiritual power of matter" (90).

Teilhard admires a friend's love of life.[6] "You must jealously guard this spirit of resistance to physical dimunition which helps you to bear suffering." However, one should not love life or the universe so much that when the time comes he cannot diminish and pass lovingly into God. As living creatures we must struggle against death, but when according to the transitoriness of things death takes us, we should freely abandon ourselves into a greater life.

Every union, especially with the greater, implies self-death. "Death is acceptable only if it represents the physically necessary passage toward a union, the condition of metamorphosis."

Marguerite: the Vocation of Suffering

Marguerite-Marie Teilhard de Chardin, Pierre's invalid sister, was his inspiration. M. Givelet has culled Marguerite's thoughts on suffering from her letters and articles in the *Trait d' union*, the bulletin of the Catholic League of the Sick, of which she was president from 1927–1936.[7]

Marguerite feels pain in anticipation. "In the difficult hours I will say to the good God that I am without courage." But at least this is a prayer (65). Elderly saints earn her admiration for they serve God without the vitality of youth.

Devotion to the crucified is essential to the Catholic

6. *Letters to Two Friends,* 1926–1952, New York, New American Library, 1967, pp. 78–79. (10/2/27)

7. *L'energie Spirituelle de la Souffrance,* Paris, Du Seuil, 1950.

League of the Sick, for Christ is in agony right up to the end of the world. This is the passion which continues right through all those who suffer. "I will never be able to leave my sickness, for this would be to abandon Jesus crucified" (74).

Marguerite believes that God gives special graces in the beginning of suffering as a viaticum. We think we are strong, but when sensible help diminishes, we find out how weak we really are (85).

A prayer during a very bad illness.

> Lord, the journey comes to a close, giving me, as others, the impression of a complete failure. I have done nothing for you: no conscious prayers, no acts of charity, nor the least work.... I have not even conquered these childlike tempers and the spiteful beasts which too often take your place in the "No Man's Land" of my sensibility. In vain I promise to do better... (96–7).

She feels so insufficient. "I have searched for you in prayer and in the service of my neighbor.... Even the actual sufferings do not afford me any joy because I support them so badly." She feels incapable of discerning anything else than her own misery and cowardice in the light of eternity.

> But perhaps also, Lord, this impression of despoiling is a part of the divine plan. Perhaps our self-complacency is in your eyes as important as tinsel and we should present ourselves naked before you that you alone may clothe us (146).

Though she feels called to suffer, Marguerite bears it badly, impatient, sad, praying poorly, intolerant. "I have concluded that I am not any more in my vocation" (149).

A sick friend, Seraphine, feels that it is God's will that she ask for sickness again. "The passion, the cross, what can we have that is better, since our Savior wanted all this for himself?"

Marguerite responds that Christ worked and taught and then suffered at the end of his life. "Do not draw, then, from the gospel the conclusion that it is more perfect to ask for illness. Christ fought off sicknesses and wept over them" (150).

Saints do not seek suffering, but rather the will of God. Look twice at self-sacrificing victims. If they are difficult, indocile, loving little, sensitive, lazy, "I would have great doubt about the authenticity of their vocation." Cultivate the ordinary virtues before taking on the extraordinary ones.

When she returns home from the hospital, Marguerite's imaginary virtues are soon put to the test. "Despoiled of our illusions, we will be more apt to understand our neighbor, to excuse him and come to his aid" (172).

Small ennuis are harder to bear than great sufferings. Day after day, the thorns of the rose, nuisances. But Christ consoles us that not a feather falls to the ground without the Father's concern.

> The crumbs of relief, the crumbs of distraction, the crumbs of solace will be accorded to us in their time, not at the hour of our need, but when the Father decides.

Christ knew the torments of thorns, nails, lance. "We, his children, ought to continue in our own poor way the redemption of the world" (175).

Winter is a bad time for Marguerite. The cold of solitude, the need of friends, the apprehension of new sorrows, doubts about a real cure, the cold of ennuis, of the fleeting years and the passing joyless youth, the cold of deception and death (178).

Little things bother her.

> This abnormal sensitivity is one of our crosses. Accept it as such, remembering that it is not a sterile cross, though it may be small. We empathize the impressions of our neighbor because we have suffered our own. And having felt the chill, we avoid giving it to others (180).

The night time is especially hard for the sick. The absence of light reminds us of the absence of God, the absence of life. Does the enemy of all consider the night an advance of his kingdom?

Marguerite is easily discouraged. Her life is finished. But it will continue under a new form.

> That which is finished is our egoism. Our plans for ourselves do not exist any more. Those of God remain and we are ignorant of them. But this ignorance and the optimism in the midst of our ignorance are the most beautiful homage that we can give to him who wants us to be happy for all eternity (185).

If God takes something from us, it is to enrich us and not to despoil us. Something greater will take the place of that which we lost. Wait in hope as the servant in the gospel. Each dawn ask. "Will this be the day my Lord asks of me?" (186).

Many complain that their garden is without flowers or shade trees. But they fail to plant the seeds left at their doorstep.

> Neither age, nor sickness, nor solitude, nor sacrifice of human love are obstacles to the work to be accomplished. If

you do not understand, God will teach it to you. If you have good will, he will come to search for you. This was the foundation of the desert (187).

We should not allow ourselves to die consciously with no care for those who still need us. If we must die, let it be an act of renunciation. "But right up to the last breath we ought to keep ourselves alert before the task always unachieved." Then death will be neither an end, nor a desertion, but the happy arrival at the home of the Father (188).

In 1950 Pierre wrote a short preface to Marguerite's book.[8] At this final stage of his life, Pierre is able to feel the total weight of suffering which seems to grow in quantity and poignancy along with a rise in consciousness.

In evolution every success is at the expense of many failures. "One cannot progress in being without paying a mysterious tribute of tears, blood and sin" (247). For every light there must be a shadow. So suffering is a natural consequence of evolution.

Christ taught us the positive value of pain by his revelation of suffering love. Though we should fight suffering, in the end it must be accepted and even welcomed. "Inasmuch as by forcing us out of our egocentrism and compensating for our errors, it can supercentre us on God" (248).

Suffering for the humblest patient is elevated until it reaches "The peak of the fantastic spiritual dynamic force, born of the cross."

Suffering well received can refine the critical senses—smiling in pain—give an appreciation of human values, compassion for the misery of others and a feeling of divine

8. Translation in Teilhard's *Activation of Energy,* tr. R. Hague, New York, Harcourt, 1971, pp. 242–249.

omnipresence and peace. "An overplus of spirit born from a deficiency of matter" (249). The Christification of suffering.

While Pierre roamed the ends of the earth in search for God in nature, Marguerite, the invalid, remained at home. Somehow her spiritual energy in God's mysterious economy was transferred to her brother. "Silently, deep within yourself, you were transforming into light the world's most grevous shadows" (249). Who has the better place in God's eyes, Pierre, the wanderer, or Marguerite, the victim?

The Meaning of Suffering

In 1933 Pierre wrote for his sister's magazine, *Trait d' Union* on the significance of suffering.[9] Illness makes the sufferer feel so useless. He or she lies there in meaningless inaction while the world is ceaselessly active, working, playing, generating.

Pierre compares the world to a large tree in which some branches are twisted and dead, some flowers wilted and some fruit infected and dwarved, reflecting its struggles against wind, snow, ice, disease, insects, parasites, birds, etc., in its fight for survival.

So also on the human level work, pain, and failure are a necessary part of the cosmic scene. Many are arrested in their ascent. "For the success of the universal effort, of which we are, at the same time, the participators and the stake, it is inevitable that there should be pain" (49).

The progress of the world can only take place at the expense of failure and hurt. So suffering and pain are not

9. In *Human Energy*, tr. J. Cohen, New York, Harcourt, 1969, pp. 48–89.

useless. Rather their victims "are simply paying for the forward march and triumph of all. They are casualties fallen on the field of honor" (50).

As the tree, so the mystical body is composed of different organs and functions. Some parts are destined to help spiritualize and sublimate progress and conquest. For example, the contemplatives and also the suffering who are driven out of themselves and help raise the world to a higher level.

> Thus it is those who bear in their weakened bodies the weight of the world in motion that by providential compensation prove the most active agents in the very progress that seems to be sacrificing and breaking them (50).

Christian resignation does not mean giving up. No, the sick man or woman should cooperate in the transformation or conversion of human suffering. There is a great energy potential in suffering. But how can it be liberated?

> The world would leap high towards God if all the sick together were to turn their pain into a common desire that the kingdom of God should come to rapid fruition through the conquest and organization of the earth (51).

Creation is completed on the cross where our suffering unites us with Christ.

Writing from Peking (1936), Teilhard speaks of the pains of personalization.[10] As the world moves towards a concentration of consciousness, suffering is inevitable.

On our way to organization we must suffer disorganization, union and separation, misunderstandings, estrangements. In the joy of growing we forget the pain, but it is

10. *Human Energy*, pp. 84–89.

still there. In order to give ourselves to others, we must renounce. "Every advance in personalization must be paid for; so much union, so much suffering" (86).

This is the pain of metamorphosis and it entered the world with man when for the first time his reflective consciousness was able to observe his own diminution (87). Death's metamorphosis appears to take us away from all that we have. But change is necessary for growth and death is a critical point on the road to union.

However, evil can be made to shrink. "The evil in evil does not lie in the pain, but in the feeling of diminishing through pain" (87). Pain disappears if we can find an achievement for which it is the price.

What can compensate man for his suffering? Perhaps a consciousness of the personalization of the universe. "Pain is virtually conquered by the cosmic sense" (89). And it contributes to evolution no less than growth.

But how can war have any place in man's progress? Teilhard sees World War II as a slipping back.[11] But even though a group of human wills falters from the course, the total of man's decisions will find the divine goal.

"Whatever disorder we are confronted by, the first thing we must say to ourselves is that we shall not perish" (14). Man's wars are crises of growth, and although evil seems to be deeply rooted, the dark troughs are balanced by airy peaks. Life "has never succeeded in rising up except by suffering, and through evil—following the way of the cross." Man's synthesis is a long and delicate process and involves many wrong turns and much pain.

Evil only repulses us if it seems useless. "Suffering and sin are the expression of the delays, the mistakes, the 'pain

11. *Activation of Energy* (1939), New York, Harcourt, 1970.

and labor' which are necessary in terms of energics for the synthesis of the spirit" (50). Only when seen in the light of evolution do they seem acceptable. Thus the mountain climber risks falls to scale the heights.

Isolated pains are meaningless. But "taken as dynamic factors in a system that is fluid and feeling its way, they are both vindicated and transfigured" (50).

Why do some suffer more than others? If the individual himself were his own end, then he would rightly be frustrated at his pains. However, if all are heading for a common goal, then it makes sense if some suffer to help the common cause. Ultimately the suffering individual will merge with the triumphant whole.

Teilhard sees war as a part of man's diminishment on the way to Omega and peace. Biologically war is the struggle for survival.

> Ultimately and fundamentally it is the divergence of the living shoots, operating from the highest level down to the family and individuals composing the family, which has always been the cause of human conflict.[12]

Peace is a steep slope to be climbed but with inevitable setbacks. It is also the point of balance to which things must eventually come. True peace sublimates war. Why does war still threaten? Man is not sufficiently purged of immobilism. He must have faith in the future.

So we should not lose hope in the midst of disaster, in the ultimate goodness of the world. When our strength ebbs, we must abandon ourselves lovingly to the current that bears us along.

12. *The Future of Man,* New York, Collins/ Du Seuil, 1964, p. 151.

In this atmosphere of blind surrender, the absurd and the unjust are transformed and take on a new meaning. Immerse yourself in a better and newer life. Perhaps you do not belong to yourself.

Do not brace yourself against suffering, but surrender as to a great loving energy. Try to rest as a seed is dormant in winter. "This is the true and great prayer of great sickness."[13]

As old age creeps up on Teilhard. he becomes more aware of his own diminishments.[14] "Stay with us, Lord. It is towards evening" (Lk 24/29). We should use the shadows, depressions, frustrations, enfeeblements, loneliness of later life. No more earthly horizons. Over the hill. But Christ, the Omega, gives us hope. For old age comes from Christ and leads to him. Alpha and Omega.

Desperately, Lord Jesus, I commit to your care, my last active years and my death. Do not let them impair or spoil the work I have so dreamed of achieving for you (100).

We have seen a glimpse of Pierre and Marguerite-Marie Teilhard's thoughts on suffering. Both are sensitive, suffering souls. Both see a positive value in suffering which is a vocation no less than health and success. Suffering is a sacrament which unites us to the suffering God and through our mysterious solidarity with other men in God we can distribute this painful energy to others who need help.

Pierre sees suffering as necessary in the evolution of the

13. *Letters to Two Friends*, pp. 104–105 (3/7/48).
14. "Retreat Notes, 1944–45," *Hymn of the Universe*, New York, Harper and Row, 1965, pp. 98–100.

cosmos toward Omega. While we strive for ultimate unity, we must battle multiplicity within and without. As a bent and gnarled tree, we, too, must suffer deformities and diminishments on our way to fulfillment. There can be no ultimate success for the cosmos without some failures along the way.

VI

C. S. LEWIS
Healing Pain

C. S. Lewis, brilliant English scholar and apologist at Oxford and Cambridge, was converted to Christianity in 1929. And he never found any incompatibility between his belief and his scholarship. As many of his contemporaries, Lewis' writings on suffering reflect the tragedy of World War II.

Screwtape

In discussing Lewis' views on pain and suffering we should first meet Screwtape or Satan who takes advantage of man's wounds and sorrows to tempt him to despair as he has done since the time of Job.

Screwtape writes letters of instruction to his nephew Wormwood, a working devil on the front lines of England during World War II,[1] reminding him that the world is still the best source of temptation. There can be found numerous auxiliaries such as the Nazis. The absence of God, feelings of guilt and anguish spread uncharity, despair, fear, bereavement.

Devils are fallen angels, creatures, and so opposite Michael, not God. Hell is on earth with dignity, envy, self-

1. C. S. Lewis, *The Screwtape Letters* (1940), New York, Time Incorporated, 1961.

importance, beaurocracy, held together by fear and greed. "Everyone wishes every one else's discrediting, ruin" (xiv). And all is covered by an exterior good manners. Wormwood should capitalize on the mutual irritation in families, for example, between mother and son. Keep each one's faults hidden from him or herself. Thus the one who is annoyed overlooks his own idiosyncracies.

The war is the devil's delight with its despair, fear, suffering, cruelty, impurity. But unfortunately some turn to the Enemy for help. They prepare for death and see their suffering as part of the divine plan for redemption. Even in pain or bereavement they can call on the Enemy.

Man undulates between body and spirit, time and eternity. But the Enemy can make good use of the troughs.

> Our case is never more in danger than when a human no longer desiring, but still intending, to do our Enemy's will, looks around upon a universe from which every trace of him seems to have vanished, and asks why he has been forsaken, and still obeys (25).

A man in the trough can easily be led into drugs or sex. And the attack is usually successful when one's whole inner world is drab and empty. Most sins of weakness occur when one is down in the dumps, with ever increasing craving for ever diminishing pleasure.

Let him think the trough is permanent, with his religious phase dying away. Distract him from prayer. And do not allow legitimate pleasures. "The characteristic of pains and pleasures is that they are unmistakably real, and, therefore, as far as they go, give the man who feels them a touchstone of reality" (40).

To keep the victim wallowing in self-pity, protect him from real pain, for real agony unmasks romantic sorrows. Make him concentrate on the past and future, not on the present where time and eternity meet. Nearly all vices are rooted in the future. For example, fear, avarice, and lust.

Make him see sex as affection so that marriage may be dropped when it wanes. Being in love is irresistible and meritorious which can lead to adultery, murder, and even suicide.

Peevishness is a favorite vice of one who sees his misfortune as injury. His legitimate claim has been denied. And the more claims he has, the more injured and peevish he is.

Middle age is a fertile field for temptation—monotony, boredom, discouragement, depression, frustration. It is hard to persevere in virtue with the gradual decay of youthful loves and hopes. There grows within a quiet despair of overcoming faults, drabness of life, and an inarticulate resentment. "All this provides admirable opportunities of wearing out a soul by attrition" (101).

Prosperity can be even more advantageous to Satan, for it knits a man to the world where he is carving his niche. Actually the reverse is true. The world is finding a place in him. Reputation, prestige, fame, self-importance. He is at home in the world and so doesn't want to leave it (101).

World War II with its tension, noise, danger, and fatigue led to violent emotions: pride, hate, fear, despair, anger. Satan notes that moderate fatigue is better for peevishness than complete exhaustion.

Once he has given in to the irremediable and despaired of relief, then dangers and gentle weariness come (109). Feed him false hopes. It will soon be over. Death and destruction are real, and spiritual consolations are merely subjective.

Human Suffering[2]

In his early atheist years Lewis had used the evil and suffering in the world as proof against the existence of God. Man suffers more than lower creatures for he can anticipate his pain and foresee his inevitable death, while at the same time wanting to live forever.

Moreover, by his superior intellect man can inflict pain and torture on his fellow men in most ingenious ways. For example, no animal scourges or racks or crucifies its fellows or locks them in caves to pine away.

Rampant crime, war, disease, terror, poverty doom mankind. Either there is no God, or, worse, he does not care. Or perhaps the world is ruled by an evil spirit whom God is impotent to contain.

It seems that if God were really good, he would want his creatures to be happy. But in fact many are sad. So God lacks either omnipotence or goodness or both (26).

Matter can either help man or cause him pain. And since matter is fixed, it cannot be equally agreeable to all (32).

Life has its ups and downs, offering opportunities for charity, but also occasions of hostility, competition, and of hurting others. Since matter is permanent, victory generally goes to those with superior weapons, numbers, etc., whether their cause is just or not. So there is the consistent policy of persecuting helpless minorities.

We are prisoners of nature's laws. "Try to exclude the possibility of suffering which the order of nature and the existing free wills include, and you find that you have excluded life itself" (34). This is not the best possible universe, but the only possible one.

2. C. S. Lewis, *The Problem of Pain*, New York, Macmillan, 1970.

What seems good to the divine goodness and wisdom may not seem good to us. But how can God's goodness be different from our own (37)? Divine goodness differs from ours as a perfect uncle's motives are superior to a child's faltering attempts.

What we want is a benevolent Father who leaves everyone do what he wants to. God is love. However, it is my own concept of love that needs correction (40).

"Kindness as such cares not whether its object becomes good or bad, provided only that it escapes suffering." But for those we really love: children, lover, friends, we would rather see them suffer than attempt to be happy in sin.

Though God loves us, he is not necessarily kind to us. Love demands perfection in the beloved. Kindness, which tolerates anything but suffering, is the opposite of love. The seeming irreconciliation between human suffering and the loving God "is only insoluble so long as we attach a trivial meaning to the word 'love!'" (46-7).

The proper place for creatures in the universe is the place God has set for them. When we want something else than what God wants, we must want something that will make us unhappy, for he gives us something we need, not what we want (53).

Love may cause pain to its object, but only if the object needs alteration to become fully lovable. Humanitarianism can be sentimental for everyone feels benevolent when nothing is bothering him.

We must recover our sense of sin and shame. Otherwise we resent God as someone who makes impossible demands, who is too negative and is always inexplicably angry (57). Once we see our badness, God's anger seems more reasonable and compatible with his goodness. We may think that we are pretty good in comparison to others. But we do not know how they relate to God.

Christians trace their suffering to Adam's sin. But is it right for man to have to suffer for the mistakes of his ancestors? We all sin in Adam. God made us good and daily we fall.

> The world is a dance in which good, descending from God, is disturbed by evil, arising from the creatures, and the resulting conflict is resolved by God's own assumption of the suffering nature which evil produces (84).

As we all sin and die in the first Adam, we suffer with the second Adam and so live.

Most of the suffering in the world is caused by man himself: whips, prisons, guns, bombs, avarice, adultery, slavery, exploitation, neglect, mental suffering. Why does God allow it?

We must surrender our arrogant self-wills to the Father as Jesus united his will with that of his Father. But we are reluctant to surrender as long as all is going well. Sin masks evil, but pain pulls the mask off. Sin and conscience can be hidden by frenzied activity, but not pain. God shouts to us in our pain. "It is his megaphone to rouse a deaf world" (93).

Retributive justice demands that the evil suffer to repair the broken cosmic order. Pain wakes us up to this obligation.

Pain shatters man's self-confidence, his self-sufficiency. It is hard to turn our thoughts to God when all is going well. When everything is rosey, God is an interruption. As long as any other avenue lies open we will take it— pleasure, drugs, doctors, etc. God is always the last resort.

God has no other alternative than to make our lives less agreeable, for that is the only way he can get our attention. But it seems so cruel. Decent hard-working mothers moan-

ing in terminal cancer. Exemplary fathers struck down in
their prime by a coronary. All they ask is a modicum of
earthly comfort and happiness. A modest home, security,
reasonable health, and a happy family.

But maybe God feels that their simple goals, a bit of
prosperity and the success of their kids, may not be
enough to make them blessed (97).

Maybe he wants to remind us that in the end all these
things will pass. The most cherished children will leave
home to build their own families and so have little time for
Mom and Dad. Material possessions such as home and
health inevitably deteriorate. Unless they have known
God, they will be miserable.

So God troubles them, warning them of the day when
they will no longer have these precious gifts. He makes
their present life less sweet through illness, sorrow, bereavement, failure, disappointments.

It is hardly worthy to flee to God only after all else fails.
Yet God humbly accepts even this paltry effort. In the end
our self-sufficiency must be shattered.

Many of our desires ignore God's will. How can we tell if
we are doing what he wants? Only if the act is painful.
"The full acting out of the self's surrender to God, therefore, demands pain," the will to obey against inclinations,
doing the hard thing for which no motive is possible.

Christ is our protomartyr, accepting his death in perfect
surrender, despite the Father's abandonment. Christ's sacrifice is repeated in his followers in varying degrees. So the
Christian is made perfect in suffering (Heb 2:10).

"Pain would have to exist in order that there should be
something to be feared and pitied." Fear and pity help us
return to obedience and charity (106).

Pain threatens our security. We go along from day to
day working well, satisfied with ourselves and our home

and job. Then disease, catastrophe, war, death. We are
reminded that all our satisfactions are really toys, illusions.
Our real treasure is Christ.

However, the minute pain is withdrawn, we head back to
our toys. That is why God gives us suffering time and
again till he chastens and purifies the soul or gives it up as
hopeless (107).

Poverty includes all other afflictions. Paradox: blessed
are the poor, yet give them alms. Blessed are the persecuted, yet Jesus prays that his disciples be spared. Pain
helps the sufferer submit to God; however, the spectator
should have compassion (110). God can bring good out of
evil. So he allows some men to hurt others. For example,
the soldier, policeman, judge, surgeon.

"The redemptive effect of suffering lies chiefly in its
tendency to reduce the rebel will" (112). Though asceticism can control passion, only God can mortify us. The
perfect man at Gethsemane wanted to escape suffering,
but was willing to submit if it is God's will.

If tribulation is necessary for redemption, it will continue until the world is redeemed or God sees that it is
hopeless. Though there is no hope for a painless earthly
paradise, that does not mean we should not try to alleviate
pain. Thus the sick seek healing even though they know
that they will be sick again.

Why does not God allow us to rest secure in this world?
Because then we would have heaven on earth and not want
to return to him (115). However, he does give brief res-
pites of earthly happiness amidst his constant reminders of
our limitations.

"Pain is sterilized or disinfected evil." Error recurs and
sin recurs and breed habits. Error and sin require undo-
ing, but not pain (116).

The evil man must not be left satisfied in his evil. Pain

wakes the rebel up to the truth. "Better for a creature, even if it never becomes good, that it should know itself a failure" (122).

The damned are really successful rebels. Hell is hell from the viewpoint of heaven. And the doors of hell are locked from the inside. Heaven is self-abandonment and union with God. Anything outside of this is hell.

The Master gives himself to creation continually in generation and back to himself in the sacrifice of the Word. "All pains and pleasures we have known on earth are exactly initiations in the movements of that dance" (153).

World War II brought a certain feeling of futility to the world.[3] Optimistic evolutionists tend to overlook cosmic futility. But there is no law of general improvement. In fact, energy tends to dissipate rather than renew itself. "Everything suggests that organic life is going to be a very short and unimportant episode in the history of the universe."

Cruelty and hostility make one doubt the morality of the universe. However, the atheist in accusing heaven of violating mercy and justice admits these absolutes on a higher level.

Not just the universe, but the people also are flawed. One out of two suffers a terrible problem: temper, jealousy, loneliness, etc. We seek outside help, but the flaws are within.

The moral law tells us what we are doing wrong, no matter how painful.[4] God became man to save man from his disapproval.

3. C. S. Lewis, "De Futilitate," in *Christian Reflections*, W. Hooper, ed., Grand Rapids, Eerdmans, 1967, pp. 57–69.

4. C. S. Lewis, *Mere Christianity*, New York, Macmillan, 1953, p. 22.

Man since Adam has tried to be his own God, striving to find something outside of God to make him happy. So things keep going wrong. "Some fatal flaw always brings the selfish and cruel people to the top and it all slides back into misery and ruin." The machine breaks down because we are using the wrong fuel (39).

Only because God suffered and died can we go through it. "Our attempts at this dying will succeed only if we share in God's dying" (47).

The Christian can repent because he has the Christ life repairing him all the time, "enabling him to repeat (in some degree) the kind of voluntary death which Christ himself carried out" (49).

When we try for virtue, we fail. So we try harder, trusting that Christ will share with us his perfect obedience to the cross.

How can God care about my problems? Certainly the sufferings and failures of billions of people must inundate even the divine compassion. But God is not in time as we are, he has all eternity to listen. Moreover, his love operates continually through his Mystical Body.

> God wants us to be perfect at whatever the cost. Whatever suffering it may cost you in your earthly life, whatever inconceivable purification it may cost you after death, whatever it costs me, I will never rest, nor let you rest until you are literally perfect (157).

God delights in our first successes, but he never lets up. Perhaps we would want to take things easy, but not to go forward is to go backward. So God gives us illness, poverty, temptations requiring more patience, bravery, love (159).

We do not see the need of suffering, but we also do not realize the heights to which we are called. "The process will be long and in parts very painful, but that is what we are in for. Nothing less. He meant what he said" (160).

Since each has his own cross, we should never judge another. Each one is a product of his own heredity, environment, temperament, and digestion. Dick's "niceness" may be a gift from his placid parents, while Joe's irrascibility and negativity may be his father's short temper and indigestion.

Christ attracts awful people. He came especially for the nasty, passionate, negative, sensual—the poor. If one has a bad heredity or environment, a sexual problem, inferiority complex, do not despair. God knows about it. You are one of his poor (166).

We are so busy pinpointing flaws in others that we fail to see the beam in our own eye. God sees all. We see all but us. We cannot repair others, only ourselves.

Grief

Late in life (1956) Lewis married Helen Joy Davidman, a widow and an ardent student of his. But their bliss was short for Helen contracted cancer which led to her painful death in 1960, which inspired Lewis' *A Grief Observed*.[5]

It is hard to suffer vicariously and compassionately for few can place themselves in the sufferer's shoes. But Lewis' bereavement gives him new insights into human suffering.

Grief is very much like fear, nervous, restless, like a mild drunkenness. A curtain separates him from the world and he dreads to be alone.

Where is God now in his sorrow? When he needs him

5. London, Faber and Faber, 1961.

most, the door is slammed shut. Silence. The house is empty and dark. Even Christ was forsaken on the cross by his Father. Is this what God is like? Why does he seem most present when we do not need him?

His thoughts keep coming back to his beloved Helen. Part of his misery is its reflection. It is not just that you suffer, but that you think about your suffering. "I not only live each endless day in grief, but live each day thinking about each in grief" (12).

His friends are tongue-tied. Perhaps the bereaved should be isolated as a leper. To married couples the widower is a death's head. "One of us will end up this way."

The separation of lovers is inevitable. Meeting is the beginning of parting. She is with God, but, like God, is incomprehensible.

She is in God's hands now. But God hurt her here. If his hurting is consistent with his goodness, then he may hurt us afterwards as well. He abandoned his own Son on the cross. He gave Helen and C. S. false hopes for recovery and then let them down (28).

Grief is like fear—suspense, waiting, pure time and empty succession. The world is flat, shabby, worn out. "Does grief finally subside into boredom tinged by faint nausea" (30)?

We cannot bank on earthly happiness, for we were promised sufferings. "Blessed are those who mourn."

Lewis realizes that he had not had real sympathy before. If he had, he would not have been overwhelmed when his own sorrow came.

Suffering knocks down one's house of cards. But we keep trying to build it up again. C. S. wants Helen back not for her good, but for his own selfish consolation. What a terrible thing it is to bring the dead back.

Helen's sins must be scoured, but tenderly, Lord. Slowly, day by day, God broke her body on the wheel. Is this not enough (35)?

God hurts us in order to heal. It is useless to beg for tenderness, for the kind physician inexorably cuts. If God is good, then these tortures are necessary. "For no even moderately good being could possibly inflict or present them if they were not" (56).

When we most needed help, God couldn't give it. Is this God's fault or ours? A drowning man cannot be helped if he thrashes around in the water, beating off his rescuers. "Perhaps your own reiterated cries deafen you to the voice you hoped to hear." God cannot speak to us if we are not listening.

Knock and it shall be opened. But no hammering or kicking at the door. Perhaps our passion destroys our capacity to receive (38).

Grief is frustrating. Lewis's habitual love impulses towards Helen have no target now and so end up in a cul de sac. She was his friend, mother, lover, disciple, counselor. Were they too happy? God says. "Stop it!" Rather perhaps their union had reached perfection and God now says, "Go on to the next lesson."

Do not the dead also feel bereavement? "Bereavement is a universal and integral part of our experience of love," as autumn follows summer. Helen is present in her absence, drawing Lewis out of himself.

God is not trying Lewis's faith for God's sake, but for Lewis's. For God already knows about his house of cards.

It is hard to get over the grief, like a man who has lost his leg and is constantly reminded of it. Lewis and Helen, though separated, are still married, still in love, one flesh, but cut in two. Ache and joy.

Passionate grief tends to cut her off. "The less I mourn her, the nearer I seem to see her." In loving the garden (Helen) he should also love the gardener (God). Loving the dead is very much like loving God, for both are absent and invisible.

God is silent in compassionate gaze. "As though he shook his head not in refusal, but waiving the question. 'Peace, child; you don't understand'" (54).

Animal Pain[6]

Can the Christian explanation of human pain be extended to animal suffering? No! Animals are not capable of sin or virtue. So they do not expect penal or remedial pain. Animals suffer pain, but are not conscious of it.

Is Adam responsible for animal suffering? Hardly, for animals preceded man. Some animals live off each other. The species of parasites are limitless.

God gave man authority over the beasts to be used or abused. Plants and animals are to serve man humbly as man serves God.

Hinduism teaches the solidarity of men and animals. Ahimsa means not only love of man, but also beasts, who are one with men in the cycle of rebirth.

Lewis also sees a relationship between cruelty to animals and men.[7] Is pain evil? If not, then there are no grounds for vivisection if its purpose is to reduce human pain. "If pain is not evil, why should human pain be reduced" (182)?

6. In *The Problem of Pain*, pp. 129–143.
7. "Vivisection," (1947) in *Undeceptions*, W. Hooper, ed., London, 1971.

However, if pain is evil, then the infliction of pain is evil. But it can be necessary for a greater good. "In saying that the infliction of pain, simply in itself, is bad, we are not saying that pain ought never to be inflicted" (183).

Pain can be inflicted for a good purpose, medicinal or penal. But it needs justification. "If a man is inflicting pain, it is for him to prove that his action is right."

In vivisection, one species usually suffers for the other. But not necessarily, for there is a growing practice of experimenting on prisoners and living fetuses.

The defenders of animal and infant vivisection say that they have no souls. Lewis responds:

> The absence of a soul (in animals) makes the infliction of pain upon them not easier, but harder to justify. It means that animals cannot deserve pain or profit from it. So all the reasons justifying human pain do not apply to animals. So soullessness is an argument against vivisection.

God created a hierarchy with man over the animals. But if man can torture beasts, why cannot angels torment man?

If a Christian pathologist is careful not to cause undue pain, his position can be defended. However, many vivisectionists are materialists and Darwinian. Those who callously use animal suffering in research, often also deny any radical difference between man and animals (184).

But if the difference between man and beast is erased, then if we can experiment on animals, we can also use inferior men in our laboratories. For example, imbeciles, fetuses, mongoloids, criminals, etc. Both men and animals are equally victims. Dachau, Auschwitz, Hiroshima, certain modern hospitals.

C. S. Lewis was a sensitive man with compassion for both

man and beast. Though suffering has a place in God's
mysterious plan to humble man and empty him of his ego,
his false divinity, his illusionary toys, to free him for union
with true divinity, nevertheless man himself should never
cause cruel and unnecessary pain in others.

VII

ABRAHAM HESCHEL
Divine Pathos

The Jewish community suffered as no other in the holocaust before and during World War II. Where is their God? Why did he not protect them?

Abraham Heschel searches the bible, the rabbis, and the hasidim for the answer. The God of the Hebrews, despite all outward appearances, is compassionate. He suffers with his people and comforts them through his prophets.

Prophecy and Sympathy

The prophet is supersensitive to evil. He may seem always angry and negative to the ignorant because he calls attention to the poverty and suffering of men. No smiling PR man is he. Whereas others see the plight of the poor and widows as nonconsequential, the prophet calls them catastrophes.[1]

The prophet takes on the pains of all. "Prophecy is the voice that God has lent to the silent agony." He is at the cutting edge where God and man meet (5). God speaks and feels through the prophet. God is concerned with man

---

1. Abraham Heschel, *The Prophets*, New York, Harper and Row, 1962, p. 4.

and is angry when man forsakes him for creatures. And the prophet echoes God's irritation. But how can the prophet be angry all the time, constantly seeing the negative side of life? Is not this depressing, pessimistic?

The prophet is always alert to hurts, as God is. "The prophet's ear perceives the silent sigh" (9). Though he seems to the complacent compromisers to be exaggerating, it is because he sees with a deeper penetration.

The sins of the individual reflect society. It is because society is indifferent to suffering and falsehood that crime grows. The prophet teaches God's compassion and justice and he warns of disaster.

The prophet is lonely, rejected by his own people. Why? They do not want to hear about suffering. So he is mocked, stoned, persecuted, called irritable, negative. "He alienates the wicked as well as the pious, the cynics as well as the believers, the priests and the princes" (17).

He is the opposite of a politician. If he ran for office no one would vote for him. No one aspires to become a prophet. He is called by God and he cannot refuse.

But the people do not want their consciences aroused or to be reminded of their sins, or threatened. The prophet's only reward is loneliness and misery. He brings God's wrath and compassion to man, standing between God and man. He has a fellowship with God, a sympathy with divine pathos.

Though God is angry at times and then compassionate, his love of Israel is everlasting. Yet he is deserted by his people as a stranger. He terrifies his people in order to save them. But the disaster he threatens is also a disaster for him, causing him untold sorrow and anguish (Jer 15: 15-17).

Second Isaiah tells us that all nations suffer in Israel and her suffering is not a penalty, but a privilege and a sacrifice and its full meaning will be given in the hour of Israel's redemption (149). Her agony is the birth pangs of salvation. God has chosen Israel to suffer for others.

The prophet fights the cheaters, cunning, humiliating, the smooth-talking politicians, those "who seek to destroy each other—with no one feeling hurt, consciously, except the victim" (161). As God, the prophet is on the side of the weak, lowly, stranger, poor, widow, orphan.

God chastises not to destroy, but to purify. Agony is the final test in which all hope and conceit are dashed and man begins to miss what he had spurned. In darkness God comes closer (Is 8: 21–9: 2) (193).

In abusing the poor we fight God himself. God with his prophet comes to the aid of the poor. His justice is self-abnegation, transitive, inclusive, interpersonal, correlating right and duty. It is like a mighty stream and to block it is to block God.

Ethos is pathos in God, and pathos is "righteousness wrapped in mystery, togetherness in holy otherness" (219). God is affected by the world. "God does not stand outside the range of human suffering and sorrow. He is personally involved in, even stirred by, the conduct and fate of man" (224).

But does not this give man power over God, if he can cause divine pathos? Man does not cause divine pathos, but rather occasions it, for his sin frustrates God. While pathos links God and man, sin breaks the bond. Sin is not a noun, but rather an adverb, a condition that can be corrected by man's return to God (229).

Divine pathos bridges the sin gap. Here divine and human meet in compassion, concern, involvement. Pathos unites the temporal and eternal, creation and creator.

Prophets do not foretell the future, but rather express God's pathos to man (231).

The Greek philosophers disdained pathos as a sign of weakness, praising apathy. They especially abhored anthropopathy in the gods. But divine pathos is not anthropopathy.

> The idea of the divine pathos combining absolute selflessness with supreme concern for the poor and the exploited can hardly be regarded as the attribution of human characteristics (270).

Where is there such a man? Certainly the bible does not see man as merciful, gracious, and abundant in love.

Pathos is insight into God's relatedness to man, not the projection of human traits into God. "Absolute selflessness and mysteriously undeserved love are more akin to the divine than the human." If man is selfless and loving, then he reflects God, not vice versa. "God's unconditional concern for justice is not an anthropomorphism, rather man's concern for justice is a theomorphism" (272).

God's wrath is an integral part of his pathos. But this is not a spontaneous outburst of ill temper, rather a proper and justified reaction to man's bad conduct. It is his righteous indignation, his impatience with evil. It is because of his concern for man that God is angry when man fails. As a father he corrects and loves, smites and heals.

And the prophets bring God's anger to the people. This is why they seem to be mad all the time, negative, constantly carping, complaining, pointing out man's deficiencies and sins. But when the prophet's abrasiveness is seen as God's anger at man's alienation from him, it is understandable.

The prophets fight apathy, indifference to human suffering. "The prophet is a person who suffers the harms done to others. Wherever a crime is committed, it is as if the prophet were the victim and the prey" (284).

The prophet screams out for all to hear that God is not indifferent to evil. He is concerned about what man does to his fellow man. And his pathos and anger mean an end to indifference. Whereas many dismiss the exploitation of the poor as a misdemeanor, God sees it as disaster.

Man's repentance can assuage God's wrath. God is not permanently angry. No, his impatience passes, but his love goes on forever (Is 54: 7-8). His anger is never final and suffering is not absolute. "Anger prompted by love is an interlude. It is as if compassion were waiting to resume."

Whereas we see crime as just an incident and the agony of the poor as a necessary part of life, we dare to call God stern and arbitrary when he is angry with our indifference.

Divine anger is not opposed to love, but an aid to it, a help to the justice demanded by true love. As Gandhi, Heschel would equate justice and love. Whereas sentimentality weakens truth and justice, anger strengthens it.

The prophet is involved with divine concern, sympathy. He hears and apprehends the divine pathos, convulsed to the depths of his soul. God's pathos gives the prophet courage to act against the world.

Sympathy means living with another person, active cooperation with God and identifying our concern with God's. In sympathy a person is open to the presence of another person and he is aware of what is happening to God.

But sympathy is not an end in itself. Rather it takes action to fight the world's suffering and to relieve the tension between God and man.

The spirit of Yahweh reflects God's pathos. The

Shekhinah hovers compassionately over the sick man. The prophet is a man filled with the spirit of divine pathos (ish ha-ruah) (Hos 9/7). He is enthusiastic, for the spirit is in him, and he is sympathetic reflecting divine inwardness. He is theomorphic, identifying himself with divine pathos in will, emotion, conscience, and message.

A Passion for Truth

The rabbis are the successors of the prophets and the rabbinical tradition carried on the message of divine pathos. Heschel discusses two eighteenth century Polish rabbis: Baal Shem Tov, the founder of the Hasidic Movement, and Reb Manahem Mendl of Kotzk (Kotzker).[2]

Baal Shem says that God plays hide and seek with man. And man gets in his own way in seeking God, because he lives in a world of phantoms and delusions. But really God is present everywhere.

"All of man's sorrow is the sorrow of the Shekhinah (God's compassionate Presence) as well. ('When man is in pain, what does the Shekhinah say? "Woe unto my head! Woe unto my limbs"')" (Mishnah) My grief is God's grief and his Shekhinah is present in my illness (32).

The prophets were melancholy people. But their melancholy enables them to see through the sham of society and come to the burial place of truth. "Perhaps it was vicarious suffering that empowered them to express the agony of sickness that afflicts us all" (207).

Kotzker asks whether man can protest his suffering.

2. Abraham Heschel, *A Passion for Truth*, New York, Farrar, Straus and Giroux, 1974.

After all, Abraham argued with God and Jacob wrestled with God's angel. Moreover, the prophets protested God's harshness and the Holy Ones opened heaven. Is it right to complain against God? R. Akiba said we are to accept suffering lovingly. "The outcry of anguish certainly adds more to his glory than callousness or even flattery of the God of pathos" (269).

Kotzker loved to protest heaven, as the sea beats relentlessly against the land. Man should not be servile even before God. "There are some forms of suffering that a man must accept with love and bear in silence. There are other agonies to which he must say 'No'" (Ex 6:7). Thus God brought the Jews out of Egypt lest they be slaves forever.

A man dressed in rags once came to Reb Mendl for consolation. His wife had just died leaving eight children. Reb Mendl told him. "I cannot console you over such cruelty. Only the true Master of Mercy is able to do so. Address yourself to him" (273).

And when a young boy died, Kotzker cried out: "Lord of the universe, what trouble would it have been to you if you let him live out his years" (274)?

Reb Mendl: "Let your heart burst before uttering so much as a moan. . . . When a man has reason to scream, and cannot, though he wants to, he has achieved the greatest scream" (281). Kotzker: "Silence is the greatest cry in the world."

Job's mistake was not in crying out in pain, but rather his silence in prosperity. Questions should be asked in both cases. Why are things so good? And why are they so bad?

Kotzker names three ways open to a man in sorrow: weeping, silence, and the highest—song. The hassid sings even on his sick bed (283). So many of the psalms are beautiful songs of sorrow.

It would be easy to say that God is not responsible for evil, but the biblical writers accepted his severity and compassion. If we accept good from God's hands, why not evil? Though God's ways seem absurd to us, to him they have meaning.

> The ultimate meaning of God's ways is not invalidated because of man's incapacity to comprehend it; nor is our anguish silenced because of the certainty that somewhere in the recesses of God an answer abides (293).

Man searches for meaning in the absurdities of life. God fights meaninglessness, finding significance in our anomalies.

Man's life is so full of untruth that he cannot see God's truth. "It is precisely the incapacity of man to share God's truth that is both the source and the object of his pain" (296).

We ask why God permits evil. But the answer is bound up with man's obligation to further justice and compassion. Perhaps the question should be: why does man allow evil? As by our sin we drive out God's presence, by our good deeds we can bring him back. "We render our modest part in reducing distress and advancing redemption." All pain is shared redemption (299). God is the quintessential Job. "In all their affliction he was affliction" (Is 63/9).

Perhaps God wants man to harass him, to cooperate with him in finding a way out of tragedy. God does not need those who praise him only when things go well. "He needs those who are in love with him when in distress, both he and ourselves" (301).

To be certain of the dawn in the dark of night. The power to turn curse into blessing, agony into song. "God writes straight in crooked lines." What seems to us absurd finds meaning in the light of eternity.

Pain is as strong as death and as cruel as the grave. But in the grave it finds truth leading to resurrection.

The divine and human need not be at odds. Man can be a partner of God, imitating his love and compassion. Does man have to be wounded for God's will to be done? Are fear and trembling the only way to faith?

When our hearts open to men's suffering, we feel ashamed of our self-centered lives. We need God's help to transcend ourselves (316). If we can but keep alive the memory of all pain and torture, who can endure in placid tranquility?

Man is the Problem

Suffering is not God's problem. He knows why it comes more to some than to others. He is truth and justice. Suffering is rather man's problem, whose untruth obscures God's truth.[3]

We tense up when we feel God's presence and we are forced to care for ends that we do not care for (71). What is important is not our despair at our spiritual bankruptcy, as the realization of our power to heal what is broken in the world. Drifting astray, we find our pole star. "Out of endless anxiety, out of denial and despair, the soul bursts out in speechless crying" (72).

God wants to be one with man, healing his alienation. All finite beings are on the border of nonexistence. So life is intense care and concern. But not only self-concern.

3. Abraham Heschel, *Man is not Alone* (1951) New York, Farrar, Straus and Giroux, 1976, p. 69.

A child becomes human by becoming sensitive to the interests of others. A stone is perfectly self-sufficient, while man can surpass himself. Self-sufficiency decreases with the complexity of form (138).

Then others become ends, not means, and we respond to their suffering and needs, disregarding our own expediency. True love of man is clandestine love of God and reviling man reviles his maker (Prov 14/31). The sense of the ineffable leads us out of self to others. We can only feel one with him in a higher unity, "in the one concern of God for all men" (142).

The bible is the story of God's concern for man in creation, revelation, and redemption. Moreover, he is present in the universe as the spirit of concern for life.

Even our self-concern is a breath of this spirit of divine concern. The world would be bleak, "if not for the breath of compassion that God blew in me when he formed me of dust and clay, more compassion than my nerves can bear" (147).

Man's needs tie him to the world and clashing needs cause suffering. He can live tranquilly while following a small objective, but when his tower totters he sees the emptiness of his short-range goals.

But man is not just one who *has* needs. He *is* a need. Am I needed, he asks. Man must serve an end beyond himself. Happiness is being needed. Who needs the old and the sick? Man cannot derive his ultimate meaning from society because society itself needs meaning.

Man wavers, ascending and descending. Our needs are temporary, while our being needed is lasting. The souls of men are the candles of God lit along the cosmic way. "Every soul is indispensable to him. Man is needed. He is a need of God" (215).

God takes our indifferent deeds and uses them to help others. For whom do we plant a tree? Divine cunning uses our instincts for universal goals (224–25). God needs man to help him achieve his ends. Life is a partnership between God and man.

Though man seeks self-satisfaction and self-fulfillment, he soon finds that these are illusions. The prophets were not self-satisfied, but went around shaking people up to come to the aid of their fellows. Life is a peril and security a myth, for the heart itself is frail and blind.

The pious man is not fooled by grand illusions. He sees life compatible with the divine. Under affliction he may feel temporarily desolate. "But a slight turn of his eyes is sufficient for him to discover that his grief is outweighed by the compassion of God" (284).

He is patient with life's vicissitudes because he sees their spiritual side. "Although the vestibule may be dark and dismal, the pious man accepts life's ordeals and its need of anguish because he recognizes these as belonging to the totality of life" (286).

He is neither complacent nor insensible, but keenly sensitive to pain in his own life and others. Yet his inner vim can rise above sorrow. In fact, grief seems to him to be a type of arrogance. It is better to love than to grieve. Gloom is "an overbearing and presumptuous deprecation of underlying realities."

The pious man does not complain when sufferings come, or fall into despair, for he knows that all is in the concern of God.

The pious man uses God's gifts in his service to help creatures and so fulfill God's concern. And his ultimate self-dedication is death.

But why is life such a problem? The fact that it is a

problem is sure: pain, bereavement, conflict, exploitation, stress and strain, wear and tear.[4] Buddha says: life is suffering.

A horse does not have a problem. A cow does not have a problem, nor does a dog worry. But "to be human is to be a problem. And the problem expresses itself in anguish, in the mental suffering of man" (3).

There is a frustration at the gap between what we are and what we should be, existence and expectation. A painful awareness of our deficiencies. Something is radically wrong, something is obscured, distorted. Modern man pretends to be what he cannot be. The great pretender. He is still in process, incomplete. His problem is not his nature, but what he does with it.

Why am I here, he asks. And he has to go through many tensions, crises, and heartaches to solve his problem. Outwardly he seems self-satisfied, prosperous, and strong. "But inwardly he is poor, needy, vulnerable, always on the verge of misery, prone to suffer mentally and physically. Scratch his skin and you come upon bereavement, affliction, uncertainty, fear, and pain" (15).

Why is man a problem? Because he is spiritually stunted. Beyond all anxiety lies the preciousness of my own existence (35).

Man's moral act is not a problem added to his self. Rather "it is the self as a problem" (36).

Man is variable, fickle, changeable, not in permanent and final form. He is inconstant, unable to remain what he is once and for all, a being in flux. A stone is final, a mountain is final, but man is never complete.

---

4. Abraham Heschel, *Who is Man?* Stanford University Press, 1966, p. 1.

Man cannot isolate himself, for it is with his contemporaries that he lives, suffers, rejoices, and dies (44). So being human implies solidarity, compassion, intuition, reciprocity. "The degree to which one is sensitive to other people's suffering, to other men's humanity, is the index of one's own history" (46). The opposite of humanity is brutality, to treat a person as a generality.

Man achieves fullness of being in fellowship, in care for others, bearing others' burdens. Being human is being sensitive to the sacred, saying "yes" to a " no."

We are tense in our search for meaning, looking for a context to belong to. We fear lest in our search for small prizes we lose the whole. There has to be an end beyond. We fear meaninglessness, uselessness, not being needed.

Who really needs man? Certainly not the earth, for it got along fine before man came. "The cry for meaning is a cry for ultimate relationship, for ultimate belonging." The earth does not need man, but God does, for he and man are partners in the struggle for peace and justice.

Man feels his true meaning only after bitter trials, disappointments, founderings, strandings. Creativity springs from man's discontent.

Man fears life because of what happened in the past: absurdity, cruelty, callousness. "A human being is a being in fear of pain, in fear of being put to shame" (96).

The world is both a problem and a task. "To be human is to be a problem," wondering, wrestling, searching, in a quandry. Is this a self-inflicted disease? And over and above personal problems, "there is an objective challenge to overcome iniquity, injustice, helplessness, suffering, etc." (107).

> In the face of the immense misery of the human species one realizes the insufficiency of all human effort to relieve it. In

the face of one's inner anguish, one realizes the fallacy of
absolute expediency . . . (113).

To be human is to lack pretenses and acknowledge our
inadequacies. Yet God needs our insufficiencies to help
him execute his wisdom, justice, compassion, and redemption.

Sometimes we feel that problems come only to certain
people. But all are patients for all suffer and have problems.[5] All feel some pain, misery, disappointment, sorrow.
"Being a person involves the ability to suffer himself, to
suffer for others, to know passion, as well as compassion"
(24).

The rabbis say: if you save one, you save all. If you
destroy one, you destroy all. But why bother with the in-
significant individual sufferer? The individual reflects the
divine. "The disease is common, the patient unique" (25).

A human being is distinct in his ability to care for others.
Care is cure and a part of the cure is to trust in him who
cures. Compassion is the mother of medicine for the
Shekhinah cares for the sick.

The physician is especially chosen to heal anguish, pain,
and affliction (28). Doctor and patient cooperate in the
fight against evil, paralleling the partnership of God and
man.

"Sickness, like sin, indicates frailty, deficiency, scantity in
the makeup of man" (32). The bible constantly parallels
sickness and sin. Sickness makes us humble, reminds us of
our neediness and leaves us open for compassion.

As sickness and sin are related, so medicine and religion
work together to heal mankind. "Religion is medicine in

5. Abraham Heschel, *The Insecurity of Freedom*, New York, Schocken,
1972, p. 24.

the form of prayer, medicine is prayer in the form of a deed" (33). The body is holy and the doctor is a priest, imitating and helping God to heal.

Old age is a terminal deficiency which all suffer with sickness, rejection, loneliness. We are ambivalent about it. We want to avoid old age at all costs, yet we want it more than its alternative.

It is easier to love smiling, affectionate young children than cantankerous wrinkled oldsters. "But the affection and care for the old, the incurable, the helpless are the true gold mines of culture" (72).

The aged are ignored as inferior, a liability, obsolete, boring, outliving their usefulness, apologizing for still living. If modern life is defined by function, what function does old age have?

There is a sense of being useless, along with one's dreams, sorrows, emptiness, a need to be needed, fearing time, escaping time into space. "Is the joy of possession an antidote to the terror of time which grows to be a dread of the inevitable death" (80)? If time is the presence of God in space, do we really fear God?

Not only the aged, but other minorities also suffer insults and prejudice. "When a heart is crushed, it is only God who shares the pain" (88). For the Hebrews bloodshed means both murder and humiliation. The Talmud says that it is better to throw oneself into a burning furnace than to humiliate a human being publicly.

While the prudent man sidesteps the issue, the prophet rushes in to ease hurts, taking others' harms on himself. Some are guilty, but all are responsible. The individual's insults mirror society's corruption. "In a country not indifferent to suffering, uncompromisingly impatient with cruelty and falsehood, racial discrimination would be infrequent rather than common" (93).

Inequality sets the stage for cruelty. It is not man who makes all men equal, but God. God is concerned for all. If one is hurt, all are hurt. Either God is the Father of all or none. So he who offends another, offends God. "The fear we must feel lest we hurt or humiliate a human being must be as unconditional as fear of God" (98). On the other hand, to cure hurt and pain is holy and takes part in God's pathos.

Man feels basically insecure in an insecure world where good and evil mix. We must help God in redemption, separation of good and evil. We keep striving for the goal, but fall back again. So there is a tension between the ideal and our own weakness.

But the state of evil is neither inevitable or final. Redemption is a long process and man's good deeds help. God wants and needs human righteousness.

We must emulate God's mercy.

> Only if there is a God who cares, a God to whom the life of every individual is an event and not only a part of an infinite process—then our sense for the sanctity and preciousness of the individual man may be maintained (161).

The religious man holds God and man in a single thought. He sees all as children of God and in loving them, loves God. At all times he "suffers in himself harms done to others, whose greatest passion is compassion, whose greatest strength is love and defiance of despair" (183).

Heschel's biblical and rabbinical tradition of divine pathos was taken up by modern process theologians to help them express a caring divinity who is affected by the changes in man's life.

VIII

WHITEHEAD TO MOLTMANN
The Agony of God

The tension between a remote transcendent deity and an immanent, concerned god has been confronted in many cultures. For example, Brahman-Atman and Vishnu-Krishna in Hinduism, Yahweh-Shekhinah in Judaism, the Trinity and the Incarnation in Christianity.

Some feel that the abstract Good, Truth, and the Unmoved Mover of Greek philosophy tended to replace the caring God of the bible in Christian thought. However, the suffering God-man of the incarnation has always been the foundation stone of the Christian faith.

Panentheism

In the 1920s Alfred North Whitehead, a British mathematician, proposed a solution for the abstract apathetic God of philosophy, showing that God receives enrichment from the world process and so is in a way temporal. Thus he can be affected by man's tragedies in sympathy and sorrow.

Whitehead sees two natures in God—primordial: infinite, abstract, immutable; and consequent: finite and conditioned by the progress of the world, temporal, conscious. In God is a sympathetic union of experiences which respond to the feelings of others. God is a fellow sufferer who understands.

God can give us fresh insights into the value of suffering.[1] He is our ideal friend who takes what is lost up into his own nature, turning evil into good. God knows evil, pain, degradation, but only as overcome by good. Every event has a finer side which introduces God into the world, saving the world from the self-destruction of evil.

> God's consequent nature is his judgment of the world. He saves the world as it passes into the immediacy of his own life. It is the judgment of tenderness which loses nothing that can be saved. It is also the judgment of a wisdom which uses what in the temporal world is mere wreckage.[2]

There is an infinite patience in God's consequent nature, "tenderly saving the turmoil of the intermediate world by the completion of his own nature." God does not combat force by force, rather he is the patient poet of the world, leading it by his vision of truth, beauty, and goodness. "The consequent nature of God is the fluent world become 'everlasting' by its objective immediacy in God."

This is an everlastingness in which the many are absorbed everlastingly into the final unity. The world and God exchange qualities, God seeking multiplicity, while the world wants unity. So God's nature is ever enlarging itself. In the end sorrow and pain are transformed into triumph, redemption through suffering.

What happens in the world is transformed into reality in heaven, which then passes back to earth. So "the love in the

1. A. N. Whitehead, *Religion in the Making*, New York, Macmillan, 1957 (Lowell Lectures, 1926), p. 153.
2. A. N. Whitehead, *Process and Reality*, New York, Free Press, Macmillan, 1957 (Gifford Lectures, 1927–28), p. 408.

world passes into the love in heaven and floods back again into the world. In a sense, God is the great companion, the fellow sufferer, who understands" (413).

Charles Hartshorne continued Whitehead's search to explain God's passibility. Only the all-knowing being can be supremely relative to all beings. So every change in relation is a change in him. Impassibility is more proper to a stone than to the all-knowing being.[3]

In panentheism, "the deity is in some real aspect distinguishable from and independent of any and all relative terms and yet, taken as an actual whole, includes all relative items."

Whereas in traditional theism and deism God is independent, in panentheism he is both the system and something different. In his actual or relative aspect he contains us. But in his absolute aspect he is exclusive (42). Can we really add anything to the almighty and perfect being? If we enjoy serving God, he will delight in our delight (133).

But does God cause evil and suffering? "The details of events—and our sufferings are among the details—are not contrived, or planned, or divinely decreed, they just happen." Their possibility is decreed (137). Suffering people are "integral members of the all-sensitive passive aspect or 'consequent nature' of the divinity, who suffers in and through all our sufferings."

The inclusive or whole being enacts or suffers all activity but does not enact or suffer all.[4] "The reflexively perfect God is a suffering God, who endures all evil, though he does not enact it or become evil in the active sense of

3. C. Hartshorne, *The Divine Relativity,* New Haven, Yale University Press, 1948, p. 77.

4. C. Hartshorne, *Reality as Sacred Process,* Glencoe, Free Press, 1953, p. 123.

wickedness." The cross is a sign of the suffering God and philosophy cannot explain it (123).

On the cross Jesus sympathizes with our troubles and sufferings and joys. "He paid the price of a bitter death rather than weaken the intimacy of his relation to the human lot, with all its suffering and failure" (147). To say that Jesus is God is to say that God is one with us in suffering.

By his sympathetic omniscience God participates in our free acts. All is within the divine sympathy, in which we are members of each other.

God is love and love is to find joy and sorrow in the joy and sorrow of others. Love is movement, action, and passion. "A changeless being cannot love, for to love is to sympathize with and through sympathy to share in, the changes occurring in the person one loves" (150).

The divine experience cherishes the qualities of all lives, for any reservation would mean shutting out from divine attention some experience of some one. Divine love is eternal, reconciling, inclusive (207).

We are contingent elements in the mind of God,[5] who experiences the unity and diversity of the world including its ugliness and discord, but there is an overall unity and beauty. "God knows and contains our sorrows and suffering, just as he knows and contains our appreciation of harmony and beauty" (42).

Though God knows the world as a whole and its ultimate harmony, despite its discord, we get only a glimpse of the ultimate harmony. Our absence from the world would have made some little difference in God (43).

God is not only the universal cause of the world, but also

5. C. Hartshorne and S. Ogden, *Theology in Crisis, A Colloqium on the Credibility of God*, New Concord, Ohio, Muskingum College, 1967, p. 42.

its comprehensive effect. He is both sower and harvester. God gave us our freedom and freedom guarantees evil, disorder, conflict, suffering. The good lies somewhere between insipid order and wild confusion.

How Can God Suffer?

The philosophical problem of the apathetic, immobile, unmoved mover does not bother the East. In recent years several Eastern authors have discussed the suffering of God in the context of the suffering and compassion of Taoism and Buddhism, and inspired by the tragedies of World War II on its eastern front.[6] Life is suffering, says Buddhism, and in the vicarious pain of the Bodhisattva suffering mercy absorbs man's sickness.

Kitamori sees pain to be of God's very essence as in the death of his divine Son (Heb 2:10). "In trying to reveal his own pain to us as human beings, God communicates through human pain" (47).

We serve God's pain by helping his Son carry his cross. So we supplement his anguish through our own, as Abraham would sacrifice his own son, Isaac.

Moreover, our pain is healed in God's pain. For if we lose our life for his sake, we will find it (Mt 16/25). He bears our sins in his agony. And man by centering his sin-associated pain in God's pain is absolved of sin.

"In the analogy of pain, man's pain serves God's pain, who completely conquers our willfullness, illusions, and

6. K. Kitamori, *The Theology of the Pain of God,* Richmond, John Knox Press, 1965, p. 26. See also S. Endo, *The Life of Jesus,* New York, Paulist Press, 1978.

disobedience" (56). God's pain and man's are joined in the
Mother of Sorrows. Human pain witnesses to divine pain
by becoming its symbol.

When man suffers in his estrangement from God, his
pain reflects God's wrath. "When the wrath of God is ac-
tualized and man suffers pain, God and man are united
through pain, the symbol of God's pain" (63).

The prophets seek God's pain which heals the wounds
caused by his wrath. "To become a symbol of God's pain is
to heal man's pain" (65).

The Suffering Servant was silent, for he knew his pain
was God's will. "By serving God's pain, the pain of the
'Servant,' though barren by itself, becomes fruitful and
enters into God's glory" (68).

Our pain unites us with God in Christ and is turned into
joy. We have died, but we will live (1 Pet 4: 13). In the
mysteries of pain we become immediately at one with God.
The mystery of the cross creates power for sanctification.
United with God's pain, our pain heals our sins.

True love is only possible in pain. Love takes delight in
sorrow, taking on the misery and suffering of others, as
Christ did for us (86). The only true sympathy is found in
the pain of God in which my suffering neighbor and I join.
But the greatest pain is when one's child is sent to suffer.
"The ethic of pain is established when all the suffering
neighbors share the pain a parent experiences by sending
his son into suffering and letting him die" (87). We can
only equalize the intensity of pain by loving our neighbor
equally to the love the Father has for his Son.

How about loving the sinner? Sin presupposes the love
which it betrays and leads to God's wrath. "The pain of
God is the tidings that God still loves the sinner who has
lost all claim to be loved" (91). Though in intense pain,

Christ still loved his enemies. The very ethic of true love is rooted in pain.

"When the pain of God loves the human condition, it first makes human pain its own, becomes one with it, and then seeks to resolve pain which is tangible" (Mt 25/40). God's graciousness lies behind his wrath. And when his love overcomes his wrath, the pain of God takes place (109).

When we are in pain, the light of God's love shines through and we are delivered from our pain by his love (113). In death God's wrath hides his love. But for the saved, death is the consummation of God's love.

The hiddenness of God is the pain of God crucified. "God the Father who hid himself in the death of God the Son is God in pain." The pain of God is the pain of the two who are one (114).

We feel chagrined when we forgive those who do not deserve it. But we forget that we are also sinners. Only God can suffer pain in his forgiveness.

God's pain is twofold. First, he forgives and loves those who do not deserve it. Secondly, he sends his Son to die. Christ separates himself from the love of the Father to step into suffering and death in order to save lost mankind, enduring the wrath of God in our stead.

God sent his beloved Son to suffer and die for our sins. So the agony of Christ unites the twofold pain of God (120).

When sinners repent and become obedient to God, he shows them his godliness through the pain of his forgiving love. By his love God once again became our Father, Christ saved us from sin and God liberated Christ from death. "Then for the first time was God's pain healed," when he received his Son back (121).

God's frustrated love pains him. But "the Lord's wounds

heal our wounds, and God's pain heals our pain." The pain of God intercepts the wrath of God so that those within the pain of God are protected. Jesus' death transforms God's wrath into his love (127).

The pain of God will precede the end. The diffusion of the gospel of God's pain necessitates the diffusion of the world's pain. When suffering is diffused, the end will come.

Man's pain must witness to God's pain. If not, it reflects his wrath. The pain of God is grace conquering sin. "The end has arrived by the coming of Jesus Christ who is the personification of pain" (143).

Kitamori maintains that the inner heart of God is pain. And we cannot see God's pain without risking death. But God covers us with his hand to save us from our fate. He wills man's salvation through Jesus Christ as his pain. "The pain of God reveals himself while saving us" (146). God's love is the victory of his pain and his pain gives meaning to our pain.

Pain turns man to God. Of itself human pain is valueless and the hallmark of fallen creation. Human pain is related to divine pain as dark is to light. Japanese trajedy, tsurasa, is closer to God's pain (148).

Though our pain shakes us to our foundation, God helps us through his pain; he saves us through his love rooted in pain. Only one who conquers pain can understand it.

Man's pain and God's differ qualitatively. Of itself man's pain is nonproductive. Darkness without light, whereas God's pain is darkness with the light of salvation. But man's and god's pain have common ground. We see that God is in pain and that the personification of God's pain is Jesus Christ (167).

It is a risky thing to behold the pain of God. Those who

have seen the pain of God are silent and speak only through the passion by bearing witness to it. Those who have seen God's pain can live without dying. For pain is also love, and by this love man's pain is purified and becomes like God's pain.

If God is love, as St. John tells us, then he must empathize with our pain.[7] The dialectic of the transcendent and the immanent in God creates tension and so the possibility of divine suffering. Divine empathy is the participation of divine passion in the world, the unity of divine and human feeling. If God is love, then suffering love is suffering God.

It is the "empathy of God, or the participation of divine pathos in the sinful world which creates in him the inner tension which is characterized by his suffering" (14). It also occasions his wrath or his estranged love.

The dialectic between the holy and righteous transcendence of God and his merciful and gracious immanence, distance and communion, rejecting sin and overcoming sin, power and glory and sacrifice. Though there is tension here, it is creative and redemptive.

Love always leaves one open to suffering. "Actual suffering takes place wherever there is destruction or estrangement of a loving relationship" (18). So God as agape is capable of suffering.

"Love is only agape insofar as it is able to suffer. And the suffering of God is only vicarious and redemptive suffering, as it is rooted in agape." Love is the fulfillment of suffering and suffering is the strength of love.

What estranges man from God's love? Sin! "God suffers only in the participation of his pathos in the world of sin"

7. Jung Young Lee, *God Suffered for Us,* Hague, Nijhoff, 1974, p. 10.

(19). Love, suffering, and empathy are united in the redemptive work of God.

Transrational pathos, "a passionate participation to love
the unlovable," God's infinite concern.

> The passionate empathy of God to participate himself to-
> tally in the lives of men in spite of their rebellion is nothing
> more than the suffering of God, which is an active travail to
> overcome the evil of the world (42).

God's eternal happiness is not freedom from suffering,
but rather the victory of his suffering over evil. Divine
suffering does not indicate any weakness or limitation in
God, but rather a voluntary self-limitation and self-
sacrifice out of love for man. Conversely, if suffering had
no effect on God, this would be a limitation.

Divine possibility and empathy is seen from the moment
of creation, an enactment of divine concern from all eternity (47). Since God participates in creation, he must be
concerned for he indwells in creation.

Far from causing evil, God suffers and empathizes it,
absorbing it into his suffering. The incarnation is the perfect expression of divine pathos, the perfect union of
human and divine experience. Whatever Jesus did, God
did, including suffering. Incarnation is the result of divine
compassion for the world.

"It was the word of the suffering God which entered in
Christ to embrace every human suffering in the world."
The apex of divine empathy is the cross. The agape of the
cross is a synthesis of the love of God and divine passivity.
We die and rise with Christ.

The eternal cross in the heart of God will remain while
there is evil in the world. The eternal cross reflects the
depth of divine empathy, the inner act of God externalized

on Calvary, the inner desire of divine love "to participate in the bottom of our existential estrangement" (59).

The suffering and death of Christ on the cross point to the eternal suffering and death of God on the eternal cross. But the suffering of God is also joy and his death prefaces his resurrection.

Redemptive love is a suffering love. So the cross is necessary suffering. "God not only suffers intensively in Christ to overcome the power of evil, but suffers continually as long as there is evil in the world" (63).

In Jewish tradition the Shekhinah is God's compassionate presence. So also in Christianity the Holy Spirit is the suffering love of the Father and the Son. On Pentecost the divine empathy of the Holy Spirit entered the church. The Holy Spirit implies the continual manifestation of God's compassionate suffering.

Christ both receives and sends the Holy Spirit. "The Holy Spirit implies also the fresh coming of the suffering God in Christ again and again until the consummation of God's kingdom" (69).

Divine compassion is reflected in the "em" of empathy, to suffer *in* another. The mutual self-giving within the Trinity is the prototype of divine empathy, as the divine suffering in the Trinity is reflected in Christ on the cross.

"All the experiences of tragedy and suffering between God and man in the world must be anticipated in the inner community of the Father, Son and Holy Spirit" (75). The suffering of the Son is also the pain of the Father and the Holy Spirit. This is the prototype of the Mystical Body. If one suffers, all suffer.

God bears suffering in order to overcome it. Christ suffers not to remove our suffering, but rather that our suffering might be like his. God suffers before we do. So he has already participated in our suffering. And because

God participates in our suffering, we suffer with him.

Christ invites us to share his cross, and Paul says that the sufferings of Christ are completed in us (Col 1: 24). Moreover, God still suffers with us despite the fact that we fail to join in his suffering (84).

Our suffering becomes a part of God's redemptive suffering, completing what is lacking in the affliction of Christ for the church. We suffer no longer, but God suffers in us and gives meaning to our suffering. So our suffering is a divine thing, a sacrament where God and man meet. Here our existential estrangement ends, becoming essential redemptive union in the suffering of God.

Theology of the Cross

Christ on the cross took on new meaning after the intense suffering of World War II and also the Christian atheism of the 1960s protesting man's plight. Though the theology of hope was popular in the sixties, nevertheless the hope of the resurrection is built upon the redemptive suffering of the cross.

The paradox of the cross. God's greatness in his humiliation. In Christ's passion God protests against man's values of pride and beauty.

Man loses his self-divinization and is given a new humanity in communion with Christ on the cross. The sinner is beautiful because he is loved, not vice versa. When atheism protests the unjust suffering in the world, a suffering God answers.

Moltmann notes,[8] "God became man that dehumanized

8. J. Moltmann, *The Crucified God,* New York, Harper and Row, 1973, p. 231.

men might become true men. We become true men in the community of the incarnate, the suffering and loving, the human God."

By the communication of idioms, if the divine nature is the center which creates a person in Christ, then the divine nature also suffers and dies (234).

The Father and Son suffer in different ways. Jesus dies forsaken. "But the Father who abandons him and delivers him up suffers the death of the Son in the infinite grief of love" (245). The Son suffers dying, but the Father suffers the death of his Son. There is division in the cross. God abandons God, yet there is a union of wills. So the cross stands between the Father and the Son.

The Trinity is a comprehensive history of the cross. It keeps the believer at the cross, apart from theism and atheism.

God's love is unconditional, taking on grief at man's contradiction. His love overcomes sin and hate. Love of enemies. There is no one "outside the gate" with God, for he himself died outside the gate (248). Beyond theism and atheism.

How can the helpless nailed God help the sufferer? The sufferer, as Christ on the cross, feels forsaken by God (252). Our love leaves us open to suffering and sorrow. "We suffer and die because and insofar as we love. . . . Where we suffer because we love, God suffers in us and helps us to endure."

> Anyone who enters into love and through love experiences inextricable suffering, and the fatality of death, enters into the history of the human God, for his forsakeness is lifted away from him in the forsakenness of Christ. And in this way he can continue to love, need not look away from the negative and from death, but can sustain death (254).

Forsaken, we are taken up into Christ's forsakenness, so we live in God and we participate in the eschaton by virtue of Christ's cross (255). As we feel his sorrow, we will receive his joy.

In his abandonment God humbles himself for man. The crucified God is in the forsakenness of every man. "No loneliness and no rejection which he has not taken to himself and assumed in the cross of Jesus." Man is taken up with his suffering and death, sin and guilt into the life, suffering and death of Jesus Christ (277). In the humiliation of the cross all is taken up in God.

Inextricable suffering, death, and hopelessness, rejection in God. God in Auschwitz and Auschwitz in God.

Modern man has been brought to the foot of the cross by war, terror, crime, injustice, alienation, illness, mental problems. Many feel that the abstractions of philosophy are of little consolation. But atheism is of small help for it makes man his own god.

The suffering and death of God in Jesus Christ make our sins into suffering and our suffering into something divine, a sacrament. The cross is our archetype, giving meaning to our suffering.

The Trinity is a suffering family. The Father mourns when he sends his Son to die, and the Son feels forsaken by the Father. The Holy Spirit, the suffering love of the Father and the Son, is left to comfort the suffering church.

Suffering does not imply imperfection in God, rather perfection, for it is based on love. In fact, an uncompassionate God would be imperfect.

IX

FREUD AND JUNG
Suffering Alienation

We have seen suffering through the eyes of scholars, saints, and martyrs who recognize a certain spiritual significance if it is somehow united to God's pathos. But what do modern physicians and psychologists say about pain? For it is their special calling to alleviate man's pangs, and most people head for the doctor at the very first twinge.

The Suffering Ego in Sigmund Freud

Freud, a product of nineteenth century positivism, sees pain and suffering in relation to the sex instinct, sadism in the attacker and masochism in the sufferer. He also feels that cruelty develops early in children, while pity and sympathy are mature acquired characteristics.[1]

In his *Instincts and Their Vicissitudes* (1915)[2] Freud notes two main drives in man, namely, self-preservation or ego instinct, and the sexual power.

Pleasure and pain are important to man so loving is the

1. *Three Essays on the Theory of Sexuality* (1905), *The Standard Edition of the Complete Works of Sigmund Freud (SE)*, J. Strachey and A. Freud, tr., London, Hogarth Press and the Institute of Psychoanalysis, 1964, vol. 7.
2. *A General Selection From the Works of Sigmund Freud*, (GS), J. Rickman, ed.. Garden City, Doubleday, 1957, pp. 70–86.

relation of the ego to its source of pleasure (GS 82). The ego strives to absorb pleasureful stimuli and avoid the painful. "The ego hates, abhors, and pursues with intent to destroy all objects which for it are a source of painful feelings." Man's very first hates arise from his self-preserving instinct. Thus hate is older than love and is a self-preserving reaction to pain (GS 84).

In his *Beyond the Pleasure Principle* (1920)[3] he says that in the ego's instinct for self-preservation the pleasure principle is replaced by the reality principle, where the temporary toleration of unpleasure is a step in the long direction towards pleasure.

However, the pleasure principle is hard at work in the sex instincts and can overcome the reality principle to the detriment of the whole organism.

Freud claims that much adult suffering is seeded in infancy where "loss of love and failure leave behind them a permanent injury to self-regard in the form of a narcissistic scar," and contribute to his feeling of inferiority. Failure, lack of affection, criticism, punishment, scorn end the child's love reveries. These unhappy experiences are repeated in later life with feelings of rejection, failure, and depression.

Freud teaches that the cortical layer is the medium of pain, assaulted from without by stimuli and from within by excitation. Pain is a breaking through of this protective shield in a limited area. The mind brings high cathexes of energy into the breach, impoverishing other areas, converting the inflowing energy into a quiescent cathexis and binding it physically.

Sex instincts are life-drives and so oppose the ego-

3. *Beyond the Pleasure Principle,* tr. J. Strachey, New York, Liveright, 1970, p. 4.

preserving death instincts. Is sadism really a death instinct which under narcissistic libido is forced away from the ego in relation to the sex object (BPP 48)?

The death instincts work towards a quiescence of the libido and external stimuli towards the primordial inanimate state, whereas life instincts increase tensions, producing fresh vital differences which must be worked off (BPP 50). There might be a parallel to Hindu karma-samsara-moksha here.

Moreover, what happens in the individual is mirrored in the moral person.[4] Thus Freud quotes Le Bon on the origins of group sadism (GS 173).

> When individuals come together in a group, all their individual inhibitions fall away and all the cruel, brutal and destructive instincts which lie dormant in individuals as relics of a primitive epoch, are stirred up to find free gratification.

Any moral person is capable of selfish narcissism, whether it be family, city, state, nation, race, religion, religious order. Any divergence from the group is seen as a threat, making waves, rocking the boat, or labeled as "negative."

Members of the group, pursuing the same ego-ideal, are one with their paradigm. So the individual feels isolated, alienated, lonely when separated from the group. Thus de facto or de iure excommunication is the punishment for dissidents who dare to make waves. Hence the great outdoor sport of "stoning the prophets," which took various forms throughout the ages.

In clan societies ostracism is the equivalent of death. "Opposition to the herd is as good as separation from it

---

4. *Group Psychology and the Analysis of the Ego,* (1921) (GS 169–209)

and is therefore anxiously avoided" (GS 194).

The herd is conservative, self-perpetuating, and self-interested. It abhors anything new, strange, unusual, threatening. So any stranger or any one with a new and different view or heresy is attacked in the interest of group narcissism, coupled with group sadism.

Freud sees group narcissism originating in the primordial horde's fear of the patriarch. So it still wants to be ruled by a forceful father figure.

Even sex must be subordinated to the group. So one may marry only with the approval and for the sake of the clan. Thus a practical or even obligatory celibacy may be required for the sake of the state, army, industry, party, church, or religious order. Here exclusive male-female love is felt as a rejection of the group. Freud, Marx, and others see exclusive male-female love as a rather late development as is its opposition to group cohesion.

Neurosis and psychosis also remove their victims from the social unit. The neurotic, in effect, creates his own group or religion. He or she is seen as singular, individualistic, odd, peculiar, idiosyncratic.

So the odd person is to be ostracized, avoided, feared as a threat, put away in homes, or kept under drugs. There seem to be parallels in society's persecution and alienation of heretics, lovers, neurotics, strangers, widows, terminally ill, aged, crippled, prophets. For example, in communist Russia dissidents are treated as insane.

From the macrocosm to the microcosm. Whereas the individual suffers in the macrocosm of society, in the microcosm of the individual, the ego is caught between the punishing superego and the id.[5] Here the ego-ideal corre-

---

5. S. Freud, *The Ego and the Id* (EI)(1923), tr. J. Riviere, New York, Norton, 1960.

sponds to man's higher nature, religion, longing for the Father, censorship, conscience.

Conscious guilt arises from the tension between the ego and the ego-ideal and expresses the condemnation of the ego by the critical agencies. The ego-ideal rages against the ego in a cruel manner in obsessional neurosis and melancholy.

In obsessional neurosis the ego rebels against guilt, whereas in melancholy it submits willingly to punishment, while in hysteria the guilt remains unconscious and the ego tries to fend off the disturbing criticism of the superego by repression. The increase in unconscious guilt can turn people into criminals.

In melancholy the superego rages against the ego, "as if it had taken possession of the whole of the sadism available in the person concerned" (EI 43). This destructive element has entrenched itself in the superego and turns against the ego. Moreover, this pure culture of the death instinct often drives the ego to death unless it can react in mania.

Obsessional neurosis is aggressive, substituting hate for love, the ego fighting against the murderous id and the punishing consciousness. "The first outcome is interminable self-torment and essentially follows a systematic torturing of the object" (EI 44).

Dangerous death instincts are either fused with erotic components or are directed to the outside world in the form of aggression, yet they still continue their internal work.

Frustrated aggression can backfire. Thus "the more a man checks his aggression towards the exterior, the more severe—that is—aggressive he becomes in his ego-ideal" (EI 44). There is a turning around on his own ego. In melancholy the superego is a gathering place of the death instincts.

The superego is a father figure. The erotic image is sublimated and can no longer control its destructiveness which is released in the form of an inclination to aggression and destruction. The id regresses and the superego moves against the ego. The ego, the mediator between the world and the id, is surrounded by danger and anxiety from the external world, the libido of the id and the severe reproval of the superego.

Through identification and sublimation the ego aids the death instincts in the id to gain control over the libido. But the ego runs the risk of becoming the object of the death instincts and perishing. To guard against this, the ego has to be filled with libido to want to live and be loved (EI 46).

The ego's work of sublimation results in a defusion of instincts and a liberation of aggressive instincts in the superego. And its struggle against libido exposes it to the danger of maltreatment and death, suffering under the sometimes fatal attacks of the superego.

In melancholy's fear of death, the ego gives itself up because it feels itself hated and persecuted by the superego. Deserted by all its protective forces, it lets itself die. There is a parallel to the ego's first anxiety at birth and its separation from its protective mother.

In moral masochism the ego is anxious since it does not measure up to the superego which reflects the parental censorship of the ego.[6] So the ego seeks punishment for its faults.

The cultural suppression of instincts holds back the subject's destructive instincts, turning sadism back into masochism. The ego is masochist, while the superego is sadist.

6. S. Freud, *The Economic Problem of Masochism* (1924), (SE 19/159–170).

The suppression of instincts increases guilt and his limiting of exterior aggression makes his conscience more sensitive. Moral masochism originates in the death instincts and corresponds to that part of the instinct which has not turned outwards in destruction.

Freud approaches suffering in a threefold manner, sado-maso, the life and death instincts, and the trichotomy of id, ego, and superego. Much of his psychology reflects the repressive atmosphere of Vienna at the time.

Can asceticism be a type of masochism? Can one suffer guilt under the reproval of his superego for real sins? Under the reality principle he can suffer for a postponed pleasure. Freud teaches that physical pain can override mental anguish, a good ascetical principle as well.

Carl Jung: The Anxious Ego Alienated from the Self

Carl Jung, as his mentor, Freud, studies the myths of primitive cultures and feels that modern man's anxieties are due largely to his ignorance of the primordial archetypes as seen in rite and story. He calls man's heritage from primal times his collective unconscious.[7]

These paradigms residing in the collective unconscious have never been acquired through consciousness and so are not individually attained, but rather passed down from preceding generations.

The collective unconscious or archetypal psyche includes preexistent forms: shadow, animus, and anima, with the central integrating paradigm called the self, which corresponds to the ego in the conscious personality.

7. *Collected Works of C. G. Jung* (CWJ), tr. F. Hull, Bollingen Series XX, New York, Pantheon Books, 1961. (CWJ 9/1/42).

Jung's universal self seems to be similar to the Hindu paramatman or cosmic self. Edinger[8] calls it the inner imperical deity or "imago Dei," which is expressed in universal mandalas. The whole, union of opposites, cosmic navel, axis of the universe, eternity, the point where God and man meet—"all refer to the self, the central source of life energy, the fountain of our being"—God.

Some see the first half of life as a developing of the ego and an increasing separation of the ego from the self, whereas in the second half of life they come back together again. However, alternations between ego-self union and ego-self separation seem to go on all during life.

The separation of the ego from the self may parallel Hinduism where the individual self, jivatman, is in a state of tension apart from paramatman, the universal self. But when the separated ego is immersed in the cosmic self—moksha, samadhi, ananda, salvation, peace, bliss.

Encounters with the frustrations and illusions of life tend to separate the young inflated ego from the self. This is symbolized by such images as the fall, exile, festering wound, torture. The ego is not only separated from the self, but it is in pain.

Jung studied the primordial archetypes of the collective unconscious in rites, initiations, mandalas, asceticisms as ancient and universal methodology of dealing with the psychic forms of life. As science tries to fathom the psyche from without, so religious gnosis seeks knowledge of the macrocosm by probing the microcosm within. The mandala is where the microcosm and macrocosm meet.

Jung seeks a spiritual solution to man's suffering. Moreover, he identifies Freud's punishing harsh superego as the psychological image of Jehovah (CWJ 4/339).

8. *The Ego and the Archetype*, New York, Pelican, 1973, pp. 2, 5.

As his mentor, Jung has great concern for neurotic suffering. "There is no form of human tragedy that does not in some measure proceed from the conflict between the ego and the unconscious" (CWJ 8/366). What was formerly bewitched or diabolic possession is now called neurosis or hysteria. But making the unconscious conscious relieves neurosis.

Jung feels that it is a great mistake to consider neurosis as something inferior, for behind it lie hidden and powerful forces. Man is born with a complicated psychic disposition which he has inherited from his ancestors—the collective unconscious, whereas the conscious is acquired individually. As consciousness and free will grow, a clash develops with suffering and tension between the conscious and the unconscious.

Primitive peoples used initiations, ritual death and rebirth, the teaching of secret tribal mysteries, to help the young boy contact the primordial archetypes and so raise his awareness of the collective unconscious.

Analytic psychology tries to resolve the conflict between the conscious and the unconscious, the ego and the self, by enriching man's consciousness with a knowledge of his psychic foundations, a Weltanschauung,

> that will help us to get into harmony with the historical man in us, in such a way that the deeper chords in him are not drowned by the shrill strains of rationalism, and the precious light of individual consciousness is not extinguished in the infinite darkness of the natural psyche (CWJ 8/381).

Kelsey comments on the patient's harmonizing union with the collective unconscious.[9]

9. "Healing and Christianity," in *Ancient Thought and Modern Times,* New York, Harper and Row, 1973, pp. 294-5.

Though this took courage, dedication, and even suffering, he found greater creativity and wider consciousness, as well as a healing influence upon himself and others. . . . Man cannot remain well, psychologically or physically—let alone socially—if he loses contact with the unconscious and its symbolic and mythological life.

Religion is the main guide for the psyche on its road to union with its unconscious source of healing.

The more egotistical one is, the more he fears death. Though his collective unconscious tells him that death is the end of all men, his conscious ego refuses to accept the verdict. "From the middle of life onward, only he remains vitally alive who is ready to die with life. . . . Like a projectile flying to its goal, life ends in death. Even its ascent and its zenith are only steps and means to this goal" (CWJ 8/407–8). The great cultures, philosophies, and religions of the world prepare for death, the universal experience of the cosmic unconscious.

Death is not instantaneous, but a gradual, lifelong process. When the child is born, it begins to die. The unconscious psyche is aware of this goal. But when man seeks to escape from these truths of blood, this only "begets neurotic restlessness—restlessness begets meaninglessness, and the lack of meaning in life is a soul sickness" (CWJ 8/415).

What is man's relationship to the collective unconscious at death? Death cannot harm the collective unconscious since it is eternal and not the product of the individual conscious ego. In a sense, the collective unconscious spells death insofar as it kills the illusion of transient things including the separate ego. Death is a return to the collective unconscious.

Jung used the deathless and symbolic collective unconscious to guide people towards wholeness through life.

The unconscious wells up in human crises, mini-deaths, in which man's ego is wounded. When maxi-death approaches, the ego wanes and slips into the collective unconscious.

When the "I" is inflated, death is terrifying, but when the ego dissolves, death is peace. Dr. Kubler-Ross[10] found that patients who guarded their egos did not accept death, but once they were able to transcend their personal existence, they willingly joined the universal self.

Jung himself experienced near death of a heart attack in 1944. He felt himself being drawn up into the universe with the earth far below bathed in a blue light. There he delighted in an ecstasy in which past, present, and future joined in one. When his doctor called him back to consciousness, he came reluctantly. Afterwards life on earth seemed like a prison. Many others have had similar experiences.

Death seems to be an astral, cosmic experience, a melding into the collective unconscious. Sometimes this may be imitated in drug states, a situation of "no-me" in which the ego dissolves.

Jung says that religion preserves the primordial truths of the collective unconscious, or the cosmic self, healing man of his self-alienation. For example, the suffering Christian flies to his healing Comforter, the Paraclete. "The Holy Ghost is a comforter like the Father, a mute, eternal, unfathomable One in whom God's love and his terribleness come together in wordless union" (CWJ 11/176).

Through this union the still unconscious Father-world is restored and brought within the scope of human experi-

10. *On Death and Dying,* New York, Macmillan, 1970; *Questions and Answers on Death and Dying,* New York, Macmillan, 1974.

ence and reflection. In Jung's quatenary view of God: Father, Son, Satan, and Holy Spirit, "the highest is a reconciliation of opposites and hence the answer to the suffering in the God-head which Christ personifies" (CWJ 11/176). He sees this quaternity in the cross, the sign of suffering based on the polarity of Christ and Satan.

"After he had experienced the world's suffering, this God who became man left behind him a Comforter" (CWJ 11/179), the great divine mother figure of the Jewish Shekhinah, God's healing breath. Jung sees the Holy Spirit as a complexio oppositorum, the apocatastasis of the dualism of the Father.

> Separated from the cosmic spirit, the soul is in pain. A psychoneurosis must be understood ultimately as the suffering of a soul which has not discovered its meaning. But all creativeness in the realm of the spirit as well as every psychic advance of man arises from the suffering of the soul, and the cause of the suffering is spiritual stagnation or psychic sterility (CWJ 11/330).

The sufferer is looking for something or someone, a Paraclete, who will take possession of him and give meaning and form to the confusion of his neurotic soul.

Since his illness is fundamentally of the spirit, the patient logically should seek a spiritual solution. However, most tortured souls head straight for a physician, hoping that their trauma is physical. But healing has always been important in religious traditions from the shamans to the martyrs, monks, and confessors. There are many healing shrines, navels of the world, where the sick one may contact the caring and curing Archetype.

Jung taught the importance of religion in healing. "Among all my patients in the second half of life, that is to say—over 35—there has not been one whose problem in the last resort was not that of finding a religious outlook on life" (CWJ 11/334).

They tend to lose touch with their roots, the collective unconscious, the primordial self, as reflected in rituals, creeds, prayers, mandalas, and mantras, passed down from antiquity. Moreover, with this alienation comes a slipping of morality and increasing tension and neurosis.

Jung himself had frequent bouts with suffering. When recovering from a serious illness, he applied his divine complexio oppositorum theory to the problem of Job (CWJ 11/ 355–470). Jung rejects Augustine's view of evil as the privation of good, since his clinical practice shows him that both good and evil are real and equally balanced. Moreover, he sees God's dual response to Job: testing and merciful.

Just as Christ is nailed to the cross, torn between good and evil, so the Christian endures moral suffering equivalent to crucifixion. However, most find the sufferings of Christ too hard, so the church lightens the load (CWJ 12/ 22).

Jung believes that in the psychic archetype, the two, good and evil, are one, and though dogma may condemn the two in one, religious practice allows the natural psychological symbol of the self at one with itself through the concepts of original sin and probabilism.

Jung wants human wholeness in his patients. They are split and wounded and he hopes to return them to the archetypal complexio oppositorum. So he introduces each patient to his own dark side, his shadow, which he tries to project on his neighbor or on a divine mediator. Without man's sin there is no need for grace or redemption. Christ embraced the sinner, two in one. So the sinner should embrace his sinful self and return to the activated archetype of the complexio oppositorum.

The tree is an archetypal complexus which evolves into the Christian cross on which Jesus is tortured between good and evil (CWJ 13/251–349). The torment is ambiguous, inflicting now the bodies, the raw material; now the arcane substance, the res, soul; now the investigators themselves who cannot endure the torments. The tree as a sign of suffering was identified with the cross of Christ with its quaternity and union of opposites.

Man's instincts reflect the primordial archetypes. Nevertheless, the tie between the mind and instinct is not an easy one, but rather full of conflict and suffering. So the aim of psychotherapy is not so much a state of idyllic happiness, "but to help him acquire steadfastness and philosophic patience in the face of suffering" (CWJ 16/81).

Life must balance sorrow and joy. Happiness itself can be poisoned if man's due measure of suffering is not felt. "Behind a neurosis there is often concealed all the natural and necessary suffering the patient has been unwilling to bear." Christian teaching on original sin, the value of suffering and the immortality of the soul apply here. But to be open to them requires a surrender to the archetypes towards an integration of the psyche.

Man reflects the primordial complexio oppositorum, a mixture of good and evil. Only by facing this can he walk the healing road to self-integration.

Freud and Jung, master and pupil, as good physicians, want to analyze and heal pain. Much suffering is generated by ego-superego tension or by ego-self alienation. In either case union with the universal self and minimizing the individual ego can help towards peace.

X

SELYE TO LYNCH
Telic Decentralization

Hans Selye: The Stress of Life

Other modern doctors have continued the battle against suffering. For example, Hans Selye who pioneered research in the tensions which bring wear and tear, sickness old age, and death. Life is stress, yet if we cannot adapt we will perish.[1]

Most diseases: nerves, high blood pressure, ulcers, arthritis, cardiovascular and renic disorders, cancer, infections, mental illness are sicknesses of adaptation. Stress is found at all ages and in all walks of life from the abused and neglected child to the wounded soldier, harried mother, frustrated business man, despondent unemployed, depressed and lonely old man.

Early witch doctors often treated illness with a general stress of terror, fever, and shock. In later times, blood letting, beating, or shock treatments were used. But how can the sting of the lash on the bare back or an electric shock cure? One's defenses are aroused.

Hippocrates first pointed out that illness has a twofold effect on the body: pathos (suffering) and ponos (toil, or

1. H. Selye, *The Stress of Life,* New York, McGraw-Hill, 1956, p. viii.

140

the fight of the body to heal itself). Unless the body struggles, there is no disease. It must maintain its homeostasis
or balance with its environment, despite damage (12).

The body and mind are constantly adjusting to stress.
When I lift weights, my heart pounds to pump more blood
and oxygen to my straining muscles. When I am cold, my
body shivers and capillaries contract to generate and con-
serve heat. And when I get overheated, my perspiration
evaporates, cooling my body.

Modern medicine can alleviate stress by nerve blocks,
arterial bypasses, drugs. There are many factors contribut-
ing to stress illness, including heredity, environment, mal-
nutrition, spiritual orientation.

Teleology is important to stress, for the responses of the
body and mind to tension are purposeful and homeostatic
(245).

When unfriendly bacteria or cancer invade the body,
there is a clash of teleologies, for these parasites have their
own self-interest. Often the patient has been weakened by
long stress leaving his body open to attack.

Man, as other creatures, reaches his optimum complexity before becoming unstable. A large section of his body
disintegrates yielding up its units for wholly different
structures, while other parts produce similar offspring.
Our complexity argues for a preexisting guiding teleology.

Stress may be fought by strengthening the body's defenses through immunization, exercise, diet, rest. Stress is
the "outcome of a struggle for the self-preservation
(homeostasis) of parts within the whole." The individual
cell in man, man in society, and the species in the animate
world.

Stress is the wear and tear of life, and the physical and

chemical changes of adaptation syndromes can be measured in adrenals, lymphatic tissues, and adaptive hormones.

General and local adaptive syndromes are interdependent. Thus a local infection can call upon the whole body for defense. But the body must consider its general good. Medical science can shake up the bodily defenses by shock, rest, drugs, and so on.

Corticoids can key one up into a euphoria, but depression must eventually come for the body cannot go on at top speed all the time. Stress tends to equalize the activity of the body, preventing the overdoing in one area through adaptive hormones.

Stress may be deviated through sports, jogging, travel, hobbies, or sublimated into higher channels.

Man's innate vitality is limited by heredity. And aging is based on the amount of stress, wear and tear of life, and self-consumption. Rest does not restore life's basic vitality. "Each exposure leaves an indelible scar, in that it uses up reserves of adaptability which cannot be replaced" (274).

But most people do not die of old age. Rather, certain weak parts break down. This is the price of our evolution into complex organisms. Unicellular animals never need to die, for they just divide up eternally and their parts live on as new beings.

Our survival is based on two main factors. First, our inherited supply of adaptive energy, and second, the wear and tear that the weakest part of our body can tolerate.

In the evolution of the microcosm, cells cooperate in an intercellular altruism. So in the macrocosm the individual aids the group teleology. Our short range failures in health or success are just minor subdivisions of our incompleteness which also includes purely passive suffering.

Long-range aims point to future gratification. This ultimate telos must outlast the moment and be earned at the price of present sacrifices, leading us through a meaningful and active long life, "steering us clear of the unpleasant and unnecessary stresses of fights, frustrations, and insecurities" (298).

There is a relationship between long-range aims and stress. Tension, frustration, insecurity, aimlessness, stress, all can cause disease and suffering: headaches, ulcers, thrombosis, arthritis, hypertension, insanity, depression, suicide.

There has to be a balance between the short- and long-range aims. The goal of life is not to avoid stress. Rather stress is a necessary part of life and we must adjust to it, adapting our energy, using it thriftily in fighting the wear and tear of our existence.

David Bakan: The Psychology of Suffering[2]

Following Freud and Selye, Bakan sees disease and suffering related to separation, alienation, and estrangement.

In natural selection the species is favored over the individual so the death of a single member may well serve the survival of the species. So in the microcosm the individual cell or group of cells must serve the telos of the whole.

As Selye, Bakan feels that the defense processes of the organism are major factors in suffering, disease, and death. Thus when the skin is cut, adjacent cells multiply to close the wound. Coagulants in the blood work to stop the flow and white corpuscles rush in to fight any unfriendly

2. D. Bakan, *Disease, Pain and Sacrifice*, Chicago, University Press. 1968.

bacteria, all serving the general telos of self-preservation. Healing pain.

However, when parasitic cells invade, either sickness-bearing germs or cancerous growth—disease. "Disease is to be conceived as the decentralization of this higher telos of the organism and its loss of dominance over the lower telē" (32), a lack of communication between the parasite and its host.

Bakan parallels this telic decentralization with Freud's psychological repression. Thus the alienation from the central telos causes neurosis and disease. And psychotherapy tries once again to bring the errant telē under the conscious purpose of the psyche.

Paradox: organic growth and development and reproduction of the species can only take place by means of telic decentralization. Thus the ejaculation of the sperm, growth of the fetus in the womb, parturition, nurture and education of the young, and ultimately the emptying of the nest. In some less complex creatures death follows shortly after the telic decentralization of reproduction. Freud sees in the postcoital ennui of humans a vestige of this.

Perhaps the fear of decentralization, centrifugation, and ultimate annihilation has prompted modern couples to put off generation either through birth control or abortion. Moreover, the dread of a rival telos may lead to child abuse.[3] Thus children can be seen as a disease which threatens parental egos.

Whatever involves separation of cells is from the death instinct, but what unites, coalesces, or coordinates cells is from eros (50).

3. See D. Bakan, *Slaughter of the Innocents,* San Francisco, Jossey-Bass Inc., 1971.

Telic decentralization takes place in all stages. In the early phases of life it reflects growth, but later, disease and death. "Death occurs because the fission-like processes continue and continue beyond a point where they are co-ordinated by the telos of the total organism" (51).

Pain is the psychic manifestation of telic decentralization and is linked with autonomous individual existence. It is basically an individual affair. "Pain is ultimately private in that it is lodged in the individual person, the person individuated in many relevant aspects out of the larger telos" (61). So pain, suffering, loneliness, and alienation are inextricably interwoven.

Pain is the burden of the individual organism separated out of the larger telos and cannot be expressed in words. However, a universal symbol of suffering such as the cross can help one overcome the loneliness and privacy of pain.

Pain is the price one pays for his conscious ego. So highly conscious and sensitive people are extremely aware of pain. Pain tries to bring the decentralized organ back into the telos of the whole.

Pain appears to the ego as something alien to it, as if the ego were a victim of external forces (74). Since the pain is an "it" to the conscious ego ("It hurts!") the ego tries to make the agony distal to itself, even if it cannot make the trauma distal to the body.

> By placing the affected part of the body in the outside world, as it were, the ego provides itself with the psychological precondition for engaging in such efforts as may be needed for reducing further damage and repairing injury (76).

Making the pain ego-alien can either fight against the telic decentralization expressed by the pain and so be healing. Or it may be willing to sacrifice the diseased part to save the telos of the whole, making an "it" of the traumatized limb. But even after the member is excised, the pain of decentralization perdures.

Pain warns us of mini-death, an incipient decentralization, which parallels and anticipates the total and final centrifugation of death. Anxiety and a sense of annihilation often accompany the pain.

Masochism inflicts pain on the self to bind the sense of annihilation to pain, thus giving the ego a sense of control over the forces of annihilation. Now the pain no longer comes from an alien force, but from the ego itself (83).

In a multicellular and multiorganed being such as man, pain can be split off from the feeling of annihilation, since the pain is localized and not seen as a threat to total decentralization. This is especially true if a nonessential part is attacked. Then the ego withdraws from the injured member, "allowing the phenomenally alien pain per se, but reserving the survival of the ego itself, and to those parts upon which the continued existence of the body is still contingent" (84).

But can the ego withdraw itself from the painful body to save itself from annihilation? This very withdrawal is a factor in its annihilation (85). We have seen earlier examples of extracorporeal experiences of dying people.

Though pain and mortality are man's tragedies, he can conquer both by identifying himself with a larger telos which is immortal, collective unconscious, cosmic soul, Atman, Self, Tao, or God. This way lies salvation, moksha.

The sacrifices of the bible, be they of Abraham or Job, are examples of telic decentralization. Bakan sees a confounding of the sense of self and others in sacrifice. Thus a sacrifice can be transitive, the offering of some one else

(Isaac) or intransitive, self-sacrificing. Something of one-self is made an "it" for the sake of the whole. Either the offering of a diseased part to save the individual ego or the oblation of the individual to preserve the collective ego.

We see this element of sacrifice in the prophet, scapegoat, bodhisattva, martyr. In persecution there is a decentralization of the dissident and painful attempts to unite him or her with the whole or else annihilate them through excommunication. They are seen as negative elements and so threats to the larger telos.

Steven Brena: Pain and Religion[4]

As suffering is found in alienation or decentralization, so many feel that the solution to suffering may be found in union with a larger telos. This is often attained through religion which literally is a binding of the soul, mind and body to God, paralleling Hindu yoga.

Anxiety is common among men who have the freedom to choose good or bad. Brena feels that prayer is a good means of calming anxiety, "a natural conscious shifting of the nervous activity from the world of relativity into the field of contemplation," where the ego fades away with the expansion of consciousness. Narcissism and egotism give way to a new wider relationship with God and others (37).

Prayer also helps break the vicious cycle of pain, suffering, and depression in the face of anxiety. Drugs, far from alleviating suffering, often mask its real cause. "The problems they mask are probably deep-rooted unconscious strivings for God" (48). Man is unfinished with endless

4. Springfield, Ill., Thomas, 1972.

possibilities for regression and growth. Drug addiction and consistent pain are nothing but cries for help (49).

Suffering and pain are not the same thing. For example, the learned pain patterns of the hypochondriac, who can keep his suffering going long after the stimuli have stopped. Learned pain habits are interrelated with the environment and the daily strain of working off real or imaginary dangers to the ego.

Though modern science has made rapid strides in neurology, human suffering still has us baffled. It involves much more than mere physical stimuli and responses.

Pain is a personal experience. We can see the motor pain indicators in others. For example, muscular, vascular, visceral, endocrinal, verbal or changes in overt acts (77). Motor and mental activities interchange. Thus mental distress brings motor restlessness. And conversely muscular work can bring mental relaxation.

But one can develop a prestimulus level of motor activity. "Because we have learned to manifest mental distress into muscular tension, we are very likely to be tensed most of the time" (78). And overstimulation leads to further tension and pain.

The vascular response to pain is most notable—paling, flushing, dizziness, fainting with a stretching of nerve fibers in the arteries and veins. High blood pressure. The viscera also are overstretched bringing nausea, indigestion, ulcers and possibly cancer.

The endocrines react in fight or flight and further responses in verbalization, sighs, moans. Changes of activity are evident, for example, long stretches in bed.

But how can any relaxation come when our thoughts are filled with desires and frustrated dreams? An anxious mind means a restless body. But prayer can help. "The

end product of deep prayer is a postprayer stable behavior, characterized by habitual calmness in body and
mind" (91).

The nature of pain involves deficiencies in sensory-
motor controls. "It may be that in learning how to achieve
self-control through prayer on his way to God, man inci-
dentally gets liberated from the agony of unnecessary suffering" (92).

Man has the capability of psycho-biological freedom, but
tends to be emotion-prone rather than emotion-master.

Spiritual and universal values can help towards universal homeostasis in which man is responsible to himself, the
social group and the whole creation.

Most illnesses involve mental factors such as anxiety and
depression (106). And often failures in unstable people are
ventilated through the sympathetic nervous system. Thus
exaggerated fatigue and low grade fevers.

Sometimes the pain vulnerable person is guilt-ridden.
Here pain and suffering are punishments for guilt (111).
This is coupled with loss of self-esteem and learned pain.

Self-esteem can only be built, "when the representation
of one's bodily and mental self becomes integrated in the
realization of our true spiritual identity" (114). Integrated
with reality, we shed our guilt and suffering in cosmic
consciousness. And our ego is given up for a new relationship to creation.

Depression, learned pain, and failure can be bridges between somatization and spiritualization. And prayer leads
the way.

Prayer behavior is the exact opposite of pain behavior
for it breaks down isolation and alienation and raises man
above his limitations and frustrations to universal values
(132).

Guilt denies the moral nature of man, withdrawing him into isolation. Sin is really ignorance of our spiritual nature, cutting man off from the cosmic stream and separating him from the archetype of creation.

Pain can no longer be considered just a simple neurological signal, stimulus/response, or a disturbing learned behavior. Rather it is a cry for total help, to function better as a member of society with spiritual dignity, healed in mind and body. Drugs are not the answer to the cry of pain for they further isolate man from his social environment.

Is pain necessary? Yes, as a warning system. No, "pain is not necessary in its misery of chronic suffering; it is an artifact of our imperfect nature" (136). It is a paying off of our cosmic debts, a carrying of the cross.

James Lynch: The Broken Heart[5]

James Lynch has found in his work at the University of Maryland Hospital that alienation and loneliness play important roles in man's suffering.

Social instability seems to produce high death rate. Across the nation instability has invaded the family with one million divorces annually, nine million one parent homes, 20 percent childless families and 23 million working wives. Birthrate is down, illegitimacy and abortion are up and child abuse and youth suicide at all-time highs.[6]

In life expectancy of the male population the U.S. ranks twenty-fourth among industrialized nations. For example, our mortality rate for heart disease in men under fifty-five

5. New York, Basic Books, 1977.
6. See *U. S. News and World Report,* Aug 21, 1978, pp. 56–59.

is six times that of Japan where there is greater social stability and a better diet.

The death rate is two to five times higher among divorced than among their married friends. Twice higher from strokes and lung cancer, seven times for cirrhosis of the liver, ten times for tuberculosis, twice for stomach cancer and heart disease, and five times higher for suicide.[7] Mental hospitals are largely filled with lonely single people.

Early loss of a parent either through divorce, death, or even work, affects the children, bringing a plethora of psychological and physical ills. Moreover, their future relationships with others are jeopardized. Sometimes their scars never heal.

The percentage of single people grows at a rapid pace. For example, in many of our major cities 45 percent of the adult population under 65 is unmarried. If you add to this unmarried youths and old people, a large percentage of the population is single.

Dr. Lynch found many patients who did not know of a single person who would care if they died. Whom to notify? Many lay in hospital beds for weeks at a time without a single visitor (155).

Many make their living off of the lonely: various types of counselors, touch institutes, nude encounters, dance clubs, singles bars, therapy groups, sex purveyors, etc. "It is almost as if we were trapped in some huge market place of loneliness, with a thousand hawkers selling different 'scientific' remedies" (193).

Loneliness is a reality of life. Most feel it at least at times. Fact: all relationships will ultimately be broken. Meeting is the beginning of parting. Love means suffering. "The ul-

7. See *Parade,* Sept 24, 1978, p. 12.

timate price exacted for commitment to other human beings rests in the inescapable fact that loss and pain will be
experienced when they are gone." The loss of parents,
wife, husband, children; the empty nest, friends move, job
changes, etc. (199).

The advocates of freedom and "liberation" say that de-
pendence on others is weakness, but this attitude only
leads to greater loneliness, with accompanying shame, silence, withdrawal, or a risky panic in search of love.

"An individual's grief, insecure ego, inability to love,
shattered dialogue, or entanglement in loneliness traps, is
also a collective problem for society" (222). Who is society?
In clan society there is a great concern for widows and
orphans. But the extended family is a thing of the past to
be replaced by a surrogate society of social workers, psychologists, counselors, and the like.

The sudden loss of a loved one leaves the bereaved all
alone. Widows are pariahs for married couples do not
want to be reminded of their vulnerability.

Compassion can hardly be commercialized so paid pro-
fessionals are poor substitutes for caring friends and rela-
tives. There has to be a concern beyond cold science and
business, coin-operated petting machines.

Loneliness, alienation, isolation, telic decentralization,
all spell suffering. But who is to blame, the isolated individual or the noncaring society?

Union with God and with all in God is the ultimate goal,
but is not easily attained in a world loaded with distractions
and illusions. If all are one in God, then they bear each
others' burdens. Is this an impossible dream? If it is, then
man is really in a bad way.

EPILOGUE

Suffering and death have been man's lot since the beginning, and he often found deep spiritual significance in them.

For example, primitive tribes used ritual torture, simulated death, and a recapitulation of tribal archetypes as a prelude to the novice's palingenesis into the tribe. Moreover, their shamans can heal because they have conquered suffering in a superhuman manner in their own lives. Later religions imitated ritual death and rebirth in circumcision and baptism.

Chinese Taoism stresses power in weakness. The soft can overcome the hard as water wears away rock. And sickness, old age, and death are parts of nature as the seasons of the year.

Hinduism sees life as a cycle of suffering in which man works off his bad karma so that he will be freed from endless cycles of rebirth and so attain moksha. The Upanishads tell us that man's separation from Atman causes tension, but when he is merged into the cosmic self—peace.

Buddha, too, saw life as suffering which he fought through nirvana (the quelling of desires), ahimsa (not harming), and karuna (compassion), based on Hindu anatta (selflessness).

In the West, Plato saw the source of suffering in the union of matter and spirit. Only in their final separation at death will peace be found. Man should practice during life for this final goal.

For Israel suffering is a punishment for sin and in her exile as the Suffering Servant she takes on the pains and faults of others as well.

Christians see Jesus as the Suffering Servant, bearing the sins of the world in atonement to the Father and making suffering holy and divine. He invites his followers to take up his cross, uniting their sufferings to his.

In modern times Karl Marx, ignoring the Christian approach, tried to fight economic traumas through counter-suffering. However, there is much pain that Communism cannot alleviate. It may bring some material benefits, but spiritual suffering, mental illness, alcoholism, frustration, bereavement, marital problems, and death remain.

Modern science has made great advances in finding the causes and cures of many diseases. Yet suffering, especially mental and social, remains a puzzle.

Suffering was attacked as an individual problem by men like Buddha and Patanjali. The group approach is seen in Judaism, Christianity, monasticism, and Marxism. Both ways are important. For example, Buddha's personal solution to suffering in nirvana soon gave way to the ahimsa and karuna of the sangha, the community. Man solves his individual problems best with the help of others.

Is suffering external or internal, material or spiritual? Before we can attain an internal quelling of desires, Buddha said, we must follow his eightfold path which includes right thoughts, speech, and actions towards others.

It would seem that suffering cannot be relegated to purely economic or social levels. Many such as Berdyaev and Jung see suffering as basically a spiritual experience, so that although many economic problems may be settled, spiritual agony may well be escalated.

Hinduism tells us that suffering flows from man's ignorance (avidya) of his true spiritual nature, his alienation from the Self (Atman) and his pursuit of illusion (maya). So most surface suffering, physical, psychosomatic, or mental is based on a more fundamental alienation from being, reality, truth, or self and a running after illusion.

This explains how we can feel joy in pain. For though his or her body is in stress, the soul is one with the transcendent and in peace.

We have seen the thoughts of many modern wounded healers, from theologians to physicians, those who have suffered and who have helped sufferers. Really all healers are wounded for all human beings are wounded, though some more than others.

Dietrich Bonhoeffer, put to death by the Nazis, sees all Christians supporting each other in the communion of the saints, the suffering body of Christ, in which they share each other's and Christ's pains. Suffering is the price of discipleship. Take up the cross. Moreover, the true follower of Christ should not just run to him when in need, but feel the abandonment of Christ on the cross.

Edith Stein, another Nazi casualty, suffered the dark night of her mentor, John of the Cross, especially in her final persecution and death in the gas chamber, her crucifixion and union with her divine Spouse.

Mahatma Gandhi in Hindu tradition sees all men as brothers. So if one suffers, all suffer. He vowed his life to the love of truth and justice.

Simone Weil, brilliant classicist and synthesizer of ancient and modern thought, from her early youth em-

pathized with those in pain, be they prisoners, or unemployed, or bored factory workers, or fatigued grape pic-
kers. Simone searched for truth in many cultures, finally
grasping it in the cross which is the holy place where God
and man meet. Wherever God and man meet, there is
suffering. She knew this in her own physical and mental
strain and her final exile and death.

Though many know Pierre Teilhard de Chardin, few
are familiar with his inspiration, his invalid sister
Marguerite-Marie. Together they found the value of suffering in cosmic evolution. Marguerite felt clearly the network of pain in which one can suffer for others. A di-
vinization of our diminishments is a part of the divine
plan.

C. S. Lewis, scholar and apologist, sees the devil, Screwtape, tempting men to domination and discouragement to
lure them away from their saving union with God.

God's love is not a weak kindness. No, he allows us to be
harmed when he knows it is good for us to wean us away
from our toys to a closer union with himself.

Is God aloof from man's grief? Abraham Heschel tells us
that though the God of the Hebrews often punished his
errant people, it was because he loved them. He had compassion on their sufferings and spoke tenderly through his
prophets.

Suffering is not God's problem, for he is truth and justice. Rather it is man's problem whose untruth and illusions obscure God's truth. Man is not just someone in
need; he *is* a need, for God needs his mind and hands to
help heal the wounded world.

Though the God of the bible is compassionate. the classical gods of myth and philosophy are aloof. Modern
philosophers such as Whitehead seek to reconcile the

abstract transcendent God of philosophy with the problem of pain.

Since God creates man and sustains him, is he not somehow related to him? Does not man make a difference to God? Does change necessarily imply imperfection? God has man's qualities in a preeminent fashion. But, as Heschel notes, compassion is not an anthropomorphism in God, it is a theomorphism in man.

Modern doctors have studied pain and suffering, using the latest scientific methods. However, they have found that these traumas are not just physical or nervous responses to stimuli.

Somehow suffering is a product of alienation, whether it is Freud's ego under pressure from the superego, or the individual sadistically beaten by the community, or Jung's conscious ego painfully separated from the primordial self.

For Selye and Bakan suffering fights against telic decentralization, whether the alien telos is bacteria, cancer, or whatever. Brena finds union with God in contemplation is a calming influence on man, something that Eastern and Western asceticism has taught for millenia.

James Lynch has proved that man in isolation is more prone to disease and death.

Is there any common theme in these modern thinkers? If there is, it is that man is wounded, incomplete, tense, anxious by himself. No one is self-sufficient. But if he is united with the Universal Being and with others in him, then he is at peace.

Whether we call the Universal Yahweh, superego, cosmic unconscious, self, or God, man must see himself as valuable to him. God did not foolishly create man out of a whim, but to help him heal an incomplete world.

When suffering comes, we ask: Why me? Rather we should put the question: Why not me? I am a human being and so incomplete. God made me and foresaw my weakness. And he constantly reminds me of this by sickness, frustration, depression, and discouragement. My toys, my illusions, my house of cards is not sufficient. I can only be complete in union with the whole self.

The solution to suffering does not lie in chemicals which mask man's incompleteness in euphoria. Rather face the pain and with God's help divinize our diminishments. Take on the sufferings of others and serve God's compassion by helping to finish the uncompleted world.

The Buddhist bodhisattva asks only to be continually reborn until he has absorbed all the suffering in the world and then, and only then, to be allowed to melt into the peace of nirvana.

It all sounds so idealistic. Rather it is realistic, for God is reality, being, truth, compassion. So compassion is reality, not illusion. And unless we unite ourselves to reality who is compassion, we are only compounding our sorrow.

Suffering is a sacrament where God and man meet. It is divine and holy since God suffered and we unite our pain to his and through his to others in a dynamic network of anguish.

For the Christian the church is the visible sacrament of suffering offering specific graces along the road to salvation. In baptism he dies with Christ in order to rise as an adopted son of God, confirmation strengthens him against the attacks of Satan. In penance he unloads his sins and sorrows on the community and in the eucharist he joins his suffering to the unbloody sacrifice of Calvary. Holy matrimony sustains him in the joys and sorrows of married life. Through holy orders a man is chosen by God and the community to represent the suffering Christ in the church taking on the sorrows and sins of its members. The sacrament of the sick gives man help in illness and in his final agony.

So the individual sacraments are specifications of the suffering sacrament of Christ in his mystical body helping vulnerable, incomplete, anxious man towards a complete fulfillment in his final union with God.

SELECTIVE BIBLIOGRAPHY

I. Dietrich Bonhoeffer, The Cost of Discipleship.

Bethge, E., *Dietrich Bonhoeffer, Theologian, Christian, Contemporary,* London, 1970.

Bonhoeffer, D., *Christ the Center,* tr. J. Bowden. New York, 1966.

———, *Communion of Saints,* tr. R. Smith et al; New York, 1963.

———, *Cost of Discipleship,* tr. R. Fuller and I. Booth, New York, 1959.

———, *Creation and Fall,* tr. J. Fletcher, London, 1937.

———, *I Loved This People,* tr. K. Krim, Richmond, 1965.

———, *Letters and Papers From Prison,* tr. R. Fuller, New York, 1967.

———, *Life Together,* tr. J. Doberstein, New York, 1954.

———, *No Rusty Swords,* tr. E. Robertson and J. Bowden, 1965.

———, *Psalms: The Prayer Book of the Bible,* tr. J. Burtness, Minneapolis, 1970.

———, *Temptation,* tr. K. Downham, London, 1955.

Dumas, A., *Dietrich Bonhoeffer, Theologian of Reality,* London, 1972.

Godsey, *The Theology of Dietrich Bonhoeffer,* Philadelphia, 1960.

Kuhns, W., *In Pursuit of Dietrich Bonhoeffer,* Dayton, 1967.

Marty, M., ed., *The Place of Bonhoeffer,* New York, 1962.

Moltman, J., and Weisbach, J., *Two Studies in the Theology of Bonhoeffer,* New York, 1967.

Ott, H., *Reality and Faith, The Theological Legacy of Dietrich Bonhoeffer,* tr. A. Morrison, London, 1971.

II. Edith Stein, Science of the Cross.

Adamska, I. J., *O Nocy Ktoras Prowadzita*, Krakow, 1973.
Collins, J., *Crossroads in Philosophy*, Ch. 5, "Edith Stein as a Phenomonologist," Chicago, 1962.
Graef, H., *The Scholar and the Cross*, Westminster, 1955.
John of the Cross, *Vida Y Obra*, Madrid, 1960.
————, *Collected Works*, K. Kavanaugh and O. Rodriguez, tr., New York, 1964.
Oesterreicher, J., *Walls are Crumbling*, New York, 1952.
Przywara, E., *Edith Stein Zu Ihrem Zehnten Todestag in 'Die Besinnung,'* Nurnberg, 1952.
Stein, E., *Werke*, Freiburg, 1962.
————, *Beitrag zur Philosophischen Begrundung der Psychologie und der Geisteswissenschaften, ein Untersuchung uber den Staat*, Tubingen, 1970.
————, *Writings of Edith Stein*, tr. H. Graef, Westminster, 1956.
————. *On the Problem of Empathy*, tr. W. Stein, The Hague, 1964.
————, *The Science of the Cross*, tr. H. Graef, Chicago. 1960.
————, *Swiatlosc w Ciemnoasci*, I. J. Adamska, ed., Warsaw, 1978.
————, "Ways of Knowing God," *The Thomist*, Baltimore, July, 1946.
Teresa Renata de Spiritu Sancto, *Edith Stein*, New York, 1952.

III. Mahatma Gandhi, Ahimsa.

Ashe, G., *Gandhi*, New York, 1968.
Erikson, E., *Gandhi's Truth*, New York, 1969.
Fischer, L., *The Essential Gandhi*, New York, 1962.
Gandhi, M., *Collected Works*, New Delhi, 1958–.
————, *Autobiography, Economic and Industrial Life, A Gandhi Anthology, Hind Swaraj. Hindu Dharma, My Non-violence, Mahatma Gandhi, The Last Phase, Satyagraha, Selected Letters, The Way of Communal Harmony*, Ahmedabad, Navajivan Trust.
Merton, T., ed., *Gandhi on Non-violence*, New York, 1965.
Smith, B., *Men of Peace*, Philadelphia and New York, 1964.
Woodcock, G., *Mohandas Gandhi*, New York, 1971.

IV. Simone Weil, Malheur de Dieu.

Cabaud, J., *Simone Weil,* New York, 1964.
Petrement, S., *Simone Weil, A Life,* New York, 1976.
Rees, R., *Simone Weil, A Sketch for a Portrait,* Carbondale, Ill., 1966.
Weil, S., *Anthologie,* ed., E. Piccard, Paris, 1960.
————, *First and Last Notebooks,* London, 1970.
————, *Gateway to God,* ed. D. Raper, Glasgow, 1974.
————, *Gravity and Grace,* London, 1972.
————, *The Iliad, Poem of Force,* Wallingford, Pa., 1957.
————, *Intimation of Christianity Among the Ancient Greeks,* London, 1957.
————, *The Need for Roots,* Boston, 1960.
————, *Notebooks,* New York, 1956.
————, *Oppression and Liberty,* Amherst, 1973.
————, *Poèmes,* Paris, 1968.
————, *Seventy Letters,* New York, 1965.
————, *A Simone Weil Reader,* G. Panichas, ed., New York, 1977.
————, *Vie, Ouvre et Philosophie,* ed. M-M. Davy, Paris, 1966.
————, *Waiting for God,* New York, 1973.

V. Marguerite-Marie and Pierre Teilhard de Chardin, The Spiritual Energy of Suffering.

Braybrooke, N., ed., *The Wind and the Rain,* London, 1962.
Chauchard, P., *Teilhard de Chardin on Love and Suffering,* New York, 1966.
Cuenot, C., *Teilhard de Chardin,* Baltimore, 1965.
Lubac, H., de, *The Religion of Teilhard de Chardin,* New York, 1967.
Teilhard de Chardin, M-M., *L'energie Spirituelle de la Souffrance,* ed., M. Givelet, Paris, 1950.
Teilhard de Chardin, P., *Album,* J. Mortier and M-L Laboux, eds, New York, 1966.
————, *Activation of Energy,* New York, 1971.
————, *The Future of Man,* New York, 1964.
————, *Human Energy,* New York, 1965.

————, *Hymn of the Universe,* New York, 1965.
————, *Letters to Two Friends, 1926–1952,* New York, 1967.
————, *Le Milieu Divin,* London, 1961.
————, *The Phenomenon of Man,* New York, 1961.
————, *Writings in Time of War,* New York. 1967.

VI. *C. S. Lewis, Healing Pain.*

Gilbert, D., and Kilby, C., *C. S. Lewis, Images of His World,* Grand Rapids, 1973.
Lewis, C. S., *The Case for Christianity,* New York, 1950.
————, *Christian Behavior,* New York, 1944.
————, *Christian Reflections,* W. Hooper, ed., Grand Rapids, 1967.
————, *The Four Loves,* New York, 1960.
————, *God in the Dock,* Grand Rapids, 1972.
————, *The Great Divorce,* New York, 1966.
————, *A Grief Observed,* London, 1961.
————, *Letters,* ed., W. H. Lewis, London, 1966.
————, *Letters to Malcolm,* New York, 1964.
————, *Mere Christianity,* New York, 1953.
————, *A Mind Awake,* C. Kilby, ed., London, 1968.
————, *The Problem of Pain,* New York, 1962.
————, *Reflections on the Psalms,* New York, 1958.
————, *The Screwtape Letters,* New York, 1961.
————, *Transposition and Other Addresses,* London, 1949.
————, *Undeceptions,* ed. W. Hooper, London, 1971.
————, *World's Last Night and Other Essays,* New York, 1960.

VII. *Abraham Heschel, Divine Pathos.*

Heschel, A., *Between God and Man,* New York, 1965.
————, *The Earth is the Lord's, The Sabbath,* New York, 1966.
————, *God in Search of Man,* New York, 1972.
————, *The Insecurity of Freedom,* New York. 1972.
————, *Israel, An Echo of Eternity,* New York, 1969.
————, *Man is not Alone,* New York, 1976.

————, *Man's Quest for God*, New York, 1954.
————, *A Passion for Truth*, New York, 1974.
————, *The Prophets*, New York, 1962.
————, *Theology of Ancient Judaism*, New York, 1973.
————, *Who is Man*, Stanford, 1966.
Marmorstein, A., *The Old Rabbinical Doctrine of God*, New York, 1968.
Montefiore, C., and Loewe, H., *A Rabbinic Anthology*, Cleveland, 1963.
Scholem, G., *Major Trends in Jewish Mysticism*, New York, 1973.

VIII. The Agony of God, Whitehead to Moltmann.

Balthazar, E., *God Within Process*, New York, 1957.
Beardslee, W., *A House of Hope*, Philadelphia, 1972.
Hartshorne, C., and Ogden, S., *Credibility of God*, New Concord, 1967.
Hartshorne, C., *Divine Relativity*, New Haven, 1948.
————, *A Natural Theology for our Time*, La Salle, Ill., 1967.
————, and W. Reese, *Philosophers Speak of God*, Chicago, 1953.
————, *Reality as Social Process*, Glencoe, 1953.
Kitamori, K., *Theology of the Pain of God*, Richmond, 1965.
Lee, J., *God Suffers for Us*, The Hague, 1974.
Mays, W., *The Philosophy of Whitehead*, New York, 1962.
Moltmann, J., *The Crucified God*, New York, 1973.
Rust, E., *Evolutionary Philosophies and Contemporary Theology*, Philadelphia, 1969.
Temple, W., *Nature, Man and God*, London, 1956.
Thompson, K., *Whitehead's Philosophy of Religion*, The Hague, 1971.
Whitehead, A. N., *Process and Reality*, New York, 1969.
————, *Religion in the Making*, New York, 1957.
Wild, R., *Who I Will Be*, Denville, N.J., 1976.

IX. Suffering Alienation, Freud and Jung.

Costigan, G., *Sigmund Freud*, New York, 1965.

Edinger, E., *The Ego and the Archetype,* New York, 1973.
Freud, S., *The Standard Edition of the Complete Works of Sigmund Freud,* S. Strachey and A. Freud, tr., London, 1964.
——, *Collected Papers,* J. Riviere, tr., London, 1953.
——, *Basic Writings of Sigmund Freud,* New York, 1938.
——, *A General Selection from the Works of Sigmund Freud,* J. Richman and C. Brenner, eds., Garden City, 1957.
——, *Beyond the Pleasure Principle,* tr. J. Strachey, New York, 1970.
——, *The Ego and the Id,* tr. J. Riviere, New York, 1960.
Jones, E., *The Life and Work of Sigmund Freud,* Garden City, 1963.
Jung, C., *Collected Works,* H. Read et al, eds. Princeton, 1970.
——, *The Portable Jung,* J. Cambell, ed., and R. Hull, tr., New York, 1971.
——, *Psychological Reflections,* New York, 1961.
——, *The Undiscovered Self,* Boston, 1958.
Robert, M., *The Psychoanalytic Revolution,* New York, 1966.
Stoodley, B., *The Concepts of Sigmund Freud,* Glencoe, 1959.

X. *Telic Decentralization, Selye to Lynch.*

Bakan, D., *Disease, Pain and Sacrifice,* Chicago, 1968.
——, *Slaughter of the Innocents,* San Francisco, 1971.
Brena, S., *Pain and Religion,* Springfield, Ill., 1972.
Browning, P., *Atonement and Psychotherapy,* Philadelphia, 1966.
Favez-Boutonier, J., *L'Angoisse,* Paris, 1963.
Fontana, J., *The Maltreated Child,* Springfield, 1971.
Fordyce, W., *Behavior Methods for Chronic Pain and Illness,* St. Louis, 1976.
Lynch, J., *The Broken Heart,* New York, 1977.
Selye, H., *The Stress of Life,* New York, 1956.
Trigg, R., *Pain and Emotion,* Oxford, 1970.
Zborowski, M., *People in Pain,* San Francisco, 1969.

INDEX